To Bless Our Callings

To Bless Our Callings

Prayers, Poems, and Hymns to Celebrate Vocation

LAURA KELLY FANUCCI

WIPF & STOCK · Eugene, Oregon

TO BLESS OUR CALLINGS
Prayers, Poems, and Hymns to Celebrate Vocation

Wipf & Stock
An Imprint of Wipf and Stock Publishers
199 W. 8th Ave., Suite 3
Eugene, OR 97401

www.wipfandstock.com

PAPERBACK ISBN: 978-1-5326-1578-8
HARDCOVER ISBN: 978-1-5326-1580-1
EBOOK ISBN: 978-1-5326-1579-5

Manufactured in the U.S.A.   JULY 7, 2017

For Maggie and Abby,
whose callings, though brief, have forever shaped my own

Contents

Contents

Contents

Contents

PART 2: WORK AND PROFESSION

Contents

Contents

Introduction

WHEN I TALK TO church leaders about calling, they respond with enthusiasm: heads nodding, eyes brightening, mouths opening to speak. Pastors and ministers know that vocation is no dry, dusty doctrine but the pulsing heart of the Christian life.

But as soon as ministers start to share their passion for vocation, I hear them name the same perennial problems, too. How can churches engage their members in questions of calling when staff, resources, and time are already stretched to the limit? Why aren't there any resources that can connect people's ordinary lives—the good and the hard—with the theology of vocation? Since parishioners are strapped for time and energy too, how can vocation become part of the regular rhythms of a community's worship, rather than one more program to try (and set aside)?

For years in my work on vocation with the Collegeville Institute Seminars, I had only a handful of favorite prayers to share with congregations that wanted to explore God's call together. Then I realized the need for a rich collection of resources on vocation was a call too important to answer with scarcity. So I decided to create *To Bless Our Callings: Prayers, Poems, and Hymns to Celebrate Vocation*—a collection of prayers that lift up the callings of everyone in the Christian community. I wanted to put practical theological resources into the hands of the ministers who could use them daily: hymns to sing, blessings to pray, petitions to offer, and sermon ideas to encourage.

But I encountered the same problems as the pastors I hoped to serve: I found few resources that addressed the joys, challenges, and complexities of callings today. So I started writing to bridge the gaps: prayers for teenagers, blessings for empty nesters, litanies for retail workers, petitions for engineers, sermon ideas for church seasons, and rites of blessings for professionals. I dug up hidden gems in denominational worship books and discovered contemporary hymn writers who celebrate vocation. Woven within one accessible volume, my creations and the contributions of Christian traditions drew together exactly what I hoped to give to ministers and their communities: the best of the church's resources on vocation and the inspiration to adapt the resources for their own contexts.

To Bless Our Callings offers practical, pastoral ways to integrate vocation into worship services, religious education, Sunday school, Bible studies, spiritual direction, campus ministry, chaplaincy, retreats, and personal reflection. Drawing from traditions in the broad stream of Christianity—Catholic, Episcopal, Lutheran, Methodist, Presbyterian, and others—the book is a unique ecumenical resource that connects rich theologies of vocation with the pastoral needs of church communities in helping Christians live out their callings in the world today.

CONNECTING VOCATION WITH WORK AND LIFE

I see vocation's possibilities, questions, joys, and sorrows sitting in church pews every Sunday. An immigrant searching for work. A woman starting a new career after raising children. A couple devastated by an Alzheimer's diagnosis. A teenager starting to date. A young adult struggling to find a first job. A teacher transitioning into retirement. An accountant wondering how best to serve his client. A newly engaged couple. A recent widow moving from her home. Given the wild diversity of life's stories, seasons, and situations, how can churches nurture, celebrate, comfort, guide, and bless their members on their journeys of responding to God's call?

Celebrating vocation starts by remembering the theological foundations of this central Christian belief. Vocation embraces who we are, how we live, and what we do—identity, relationships, and work. As a theological concept, vocation has now expanded beyond traditional definitions of ordained ministry to include diverse ways God calls people within their particular circumstances. It embraces how to find meaning and purpose in work and relationships, how to balance multiple responsibilities, how to connect personal concerns to the common good, how to listen deeply to God, and how to respond with faith and courage.

Yet many Christians do not believe they have a calling.

Many people report finding purpose and meaning in their work, family, and relationships. But even those who are highly involved in churches often struggle to relate who they are or what they do with a calling from God. Why does this disconnect exist? One reason is language. When Christians are asked to describe their lives in relationship to God, theological terms like *vocation* fall flat. Ironically, bookstores' self-help and inspirational sections overflow with new titles on "meaning," "purpose," and "fulfillment." The concept of calling is no longer religious, and therefore most Christians do not see their lives as a response to God as caller.

Another reason for the deep disconnect is that people do not belong to communities of calling. They rarely hear the joys and challenges of their vocations addressed in sermons or in prayer during worship. They seldom receive a blessing for being an accountant, a truck driver, a college student, or a new grandmother. Most congregations lack ways for members to explore their work or relationships as callings—leaving many Christians who long to understand God's call for their lives to figure it out alone.

Where vocation is neglected, the church is diminished. When questions of calling are left in church pews unnoticed, people stop showing up.

But congregations that celebrate and support people's callings can help connect their lives to God's work in the world and the flourishing of the common good. Vocation is not simply a subject for a one-time sermon or even a six-week series—it is a matter of life and death for the survival of the church and for the thriving of its people.

HOW TO BLESS CALLINGS

Through prayer, poetry, and sacred song, *To Bless Our Callings* speaks to the heart of vocation's richness. This book is intended for use primarily by pastors and ministers for your planning of worship and other aspects of congregational and community life. It has three main parts. Part 1 (Ages and Stages) gathers worship resources for childhood, adolescence, young adulthood, middle adulthood, later adulthood, and older adulthood:

- prayers to mark milestones and everyday moments
- blessings for times and places of congregational welcome
- petitions for particular needs, griefs, and losses
- hymns and poems with themes related to each lifespan stage

Part 2 (Work and Profession) offers resources that speak to work as a calling:

- prayers for work and unemployment
- petitions and prayers for particular professions
- a ritual of blessing that can be adapted for use with any professional group

Part 3 (A Year of Blessing) highlights moments to pray and preach about calling throughout the liturgical and secular calendars, to inspire your preaching and connect themes from church feasts and cultural holidays with the stories of vocation in your congregation.

To Bless Our Callings includes prayers to lift up the general calling shared by all Christians: our common call to discipleship as followers of Christ. It also offers unique blessings that speak to particular callings: the diverse ways that people are called to their work, relationships, and other forms of service. Half of the prayers and blessings in the book were written by me, drawing from the theological work on vocation from the Collegeville Institute Seminars (see the appendix to learn more). Half were collected from a broad range of denominational and pastoral resources. To accommodate an ecumenical audience, Scripture references are taken from the New Revised Standard Version, a widely accepted translation. As you use these resources within your own ministry context, you may be encouraged—as I have been—to discover how deeply the central claims of vocation resonate across Christian traditions.

CELEBRATING CALLING IN COMMUNITY

To Bless Our Callings aims to help you start conversations about vocation with the people you serve. This is how churches become communities of calling: by blessing, celebrating, and supporting the vocations of all. *To Bless Our Callings* is intended to offer creative inspiration for your own ministry. As I have done throughout this book, you may find that you need to create your own prayers on calling or adapt existing prayers to serve your context. While the volume covers the lifespan from birth to death and celebrates a wide variety of work that people do, it is meant to be evocative, not exhaustive. By illustrating the diversity and complexity of callings, I hope to equip and inspire you as a minister to bless, pray, sing, and preach about vocation throughout the year.

People today are hungry to have their personal and professional identities affirmed by their faith communities. They long to share stories of struggle and joy related to God's work in their lives. So when churches start nurturing the callings of all their members, powerful transformations can happen. Your vocation as a minister invites you to lift up the callings of all people and walk with them on their journeys of faith—no matter their age, profession, or stage of life. May your own sense of vocation be strengthened as you celebrate God at work in the lives of those you are called to serve.

PART 1

Ages and Stages

O God, from my youth you have taught me,

and I still proclaim your wondrous deeds.

So even to old age and gray hairs,

O God, do not forsake me,

until I proclaim your might

to all the generations to come.

—Ps 71:17–18

PART 1 OF *To Bless Our Callings* offers prayers, poems, and hymns for use in ministry with people across the lifespan. Chapters 1 through 6 honor the particular joys, struggles, challenges, and gifts of each stage: childhood, adolescence, young adulthood, middle adulthood, later adulthood, and older adulthood. A final chapter offers a collection of general resources that speak to the callings of the whole lifespan across generations, including prayers for weddings and funerals.

1

Prayers for Childhood

To CELEBRATE CALLINGS, LET us start at the beginning—with the youngest. Children have vocations. They are not simply on the way to becoming a teenager and then an adult; they are called by God as the children they are today. From an early age, children can experience God's presence—in nature, at play, or in church—in ways that lead them to feel connected to the divine. This connection can lead to a strong sense of being called to a particular kind of work, role, or relationship. When invited to share stories about their sense of calling, adults often remember childhood as a fertile time for vocational exploration, experience, and imagination.

Children's sense of calling emerges in a variety of ways. First, they have a deep capacity for faith and wonder. By their smaller size and their fresh perspectives, they see things differently than adults, and they ask big questions about the world around them. Second, children have particular gifts that emerge at home, school, or church. If nurtured in childhood, these gifts can lead to a path to follow toward work and service in the future. Third, children have particular callings to be sons and daughters, siblings and students, friends and neighbors, and members of faith communities. Through these roles and relationships, children call forth the callings of adults in turn—to be parents and grandparents, aunts and uncles, teachers and neighbors, coaches and caregivers.

Communities that welcome children and their callings challenge popular misconceptions that vocation is only about paid work in adulthood. By noticing and nurturing the gifts of children in its midst, your congregation can bear prophetic witness to calling as the fundamental relationship between humans and God from the beginning of our lives.

BLESSINGS FOR MOMENTS AND MILESTONES

A General Blessing for the Callings of Children

The following blessing for the calling of children (based on 1 Sam 3) can be prayed before or after a children's sermon, or when the Scripture readings for the day speak about children.

> God our caller,
> You woke Samuel in the night with your call.
> Help children to listen for your call in their lives.
>
> You filled Samuel's heart with questions and wonder.
> Open the eyes and ears of children to see and hear your ways.
>
> You led Eli to help Samuel understand your words.
> Let us listen to the voices of children as we seek to guide them in
>   faith.
>
> You remained with Samuel as he grew.
> Bless children as they grow through work and play.
>
> Help all of us gathered here, young and old,
> to respond to your call with trust
> as we echo Samuel's words:
> "Speak, Lord, your servant is listening."
>
> Amen.

A Blessing for the Child in the Womb

A new calling is created with the beginning of each new life. The prophet Jeremiah believed God called him before his birth: "Before I formed you in the womb I knew you, and before you were born I consecrated you" (Jer 1:5). The psalmist speaks of God like a weaver who "knit me together in my mother's womb . . . intricately woven in the depths of the earth" (Ps 139:13, 15). The following blessing for a child in the womb can be prayed at baptism preparation classes, in parents' groups, or at home by the parents themselves.

> Creator God,
> You knit each life together
> in the sacred dark of the womb,
> weaving a new calling.
>
> You breathe your Spirit
> into each new life,
> filling body and soul with love.
>
> Bless this baby who grows each day and night,
> whose life is still a mystery,
> whose vocation will unfold before our eyes.
>
> Help us to welcome this child with love
> and to let our lives be changed
> by all that this child will call forth from us.
>
> Amen.

Part 1: Ages and Stages

A Blessing after Birth

Celebrating childbirth as a vocational experience frames this life-changing transition as a powerful encounter with God's presence—not only for the child but also for the parents, grandparents, other relatives, and caregivers. This blessing after the birth of a child can be prayed in the hospital, at home, within Sunday worship, or in other gatherings with new parents. (For children welcomed by adoption or foster care, change the word *birth* to *adoption, arrival,* or other appropriate term.)

God of Life,
We thank you for the life of this child, *N.*
for *her* safe arrival into the arms of *her* parents.

May their joy at the *birth* of their *daughter*
increase with wonder
at each moment and milestone of *her* first year.
Help *N.'s* parents to believe,
even during long days and sleepless nights,
that they are planting seeds of love and trust
that will bloom in time.

Bless *N.'s* parents and grandparents, *brothers* and *sisters*, friends and family,
as they rejoice in welcoming this new love into their lives.
Bless the caregivers, teachers, doctors, and nurses
who will comfort and care for *N.* as *she* grows.
Let all of us share in their calling
to help raise and nurture *N.*
May we respond to *her* needs,
encourage *her* gifts,
and welcome *her* in your name
as a member of our community,
called by God.

Amen.

A Blessing at Baptism

Baptism marks a Christian's initiation into a community of disciples who share a common calling to follow Christ. While your tradition has its particular rites for baptism, you may wish to add the following blessing to the end of the service as a sending forth of the newly baptized child and the community called to care for its newest member.

God of new life,
Bless this newly baptized child, *N.*
called to follow Christ.

Grant that as *N.* awakens
to the brokenness and beauty of our world,
he will be strengthened by the grace of baptism
to bring hope where there is doubt,
love where there is hate,
and peace where there is fear.

Guide *N.'s* feet
to walk in the path of discipleship.
Bless *his* way
with wise companions and gentle guides.
Call forth *his* gifts
to serve the common good,
as you call each of us
to give our lives in love.

As we go forth from this place,
holding *N.* in our prayers,
help us to hold in our hearts
the hope of this day,
remembering our own call to follow Christ.
Deepen the faith of our community
that we might bear witness to the promises of baptism,
strengthened by your Spirit. Amen.

A Blessing for Welcoming Children to the Lord's Supper

Each time a congregation gathers around the table, we remember our need for nourishment to sustain our callings. Whenever the community celebrates the moment of a child's first participation in the Lord's Supper, the moment is an important step in the child's vocational journey. This blessing can be offered after communion, at a special gathering following the service, or at home with the child's family.

God of goodness,

When Jesus blessed food to feed the thousands,
it was a child who first brought forth
the loaves and fishes he had to share.
Let us receive the gifts of children with open arms,
that our whole community might be fed
from their love and laughter.
Bless the children who receive communion
for the first time today.
May they always be nourished by your love
and strengthened to carry out your call
to serve the hungry world as Jesus did.
May all of us gathered in this place
let ourselves be poured out
in service of our callings.
May our lives be blessed
by the communion of your love. Amen.

A Blessing for a New School Year for Elementary Students

The call to be a student is a central part of childhood. The opening of a new school year provides a fitting moment to bless the vocations of children as students. To include the voices of children in worship, you may invite a group of children to lead this prayer by each taking one line of the litany.

God of love,
May your Spirit guide us as we start a new school year.

We are called to be students.
Bless our learning and growing, at home and at school.

We are called to be friends.
Help us to care for each other, with kindness and compassion.

We are called to be leaders.
Bless our listening and speaking, in our classrooms and communities.

We are called to be followers.
Help us to live out our faith in Christ, no matter where we go.

May we greet each new day as a chance to learn and grow
in faith and love for you, who calls each of us by name.

In Jesus's name we pray,
Amen.

PRAYERS FOR TIMES AND PLACES OF WELCOME

Following the witness of Jesus who welcomed and blessed children, Christians are invited to see care for children as a communal concern and a vital part of the church's mission. One way to honor the vocations of children is to pray over the times and places where children gather at your church: in the nursery, in classrooms, and at camps.

A Prayer for the Nursery

The church nursery offers a perfect place to bless the callings of children: "Whoever welcomes this child in my name welcomes me, and whoever welcomes me welcomes the one who sent me; for the least among all of you is the greatest" (Luke 9:48). This prayer for the nursery can be used to bless children and their caregivers. It can also be posted on the nursery wall to remind all who enter that this room is a sacred space.

> God who shepherds the lambs and cares for the least,
> Bless the children who play and learn in this place.
> Grant patience and joy to their caregivers.
> Keep these children safe and secure in their care.
>
> May this sacred space be a place
> where children learn about God's love and listen for God's call.
> May our community always hold these children in prayer
> and welcome their gifts in your name.
>
> We pray in the name of Jesus, your child.
> Amen.

A Prayer for Sunday School or Religious Education Classes

Children need wise, caring adults to instruct and guide them, especially as they explore the big questions that children are unafraid to ask. This prayer for Sunday school or religious education classes can be prayed by teachers and students at the beginning of each class or during catechists' meetings.

God of wisdom and wonder,
Help us learn from each other
as we learn about you.
Speak your truth to our hearts.
Shine your light on our questions.
Guide our searching and seeking.
Direct our thoughts and efforts
to work together in your name.
Let us encourage each other
as we work toward your reign of justice
and forgive one another
as we walk on the way of discipleship.
Help us to love those you call us to love.
Amen.

A Prayer for Vacation Bible School or Summer Camp

Summer programs like vacation Bible school or church camps offer creative opportunities to encourage children in their Christian callings through songs, games, skits, and crafts. This blessing can be prayed at the beginning or end of each day, or in the weeks of preparation by staff and lay leaders.

God of delight,
Bless our week together,
our playing, singing, learning, and creating together.
Open our ears to hear your word.
Open our eyes to see the needs of our world.
Open our hearts to serve with love.
May we grow in love for you and for each other
as we listen to your call in our lives.
Amen.

PETITIONS FOR THE CALLINGS OF CHILDHOOD

Including the cares and concerns of children within worship acknowledges their full personhood and expands the community's circle of prayer to embrace its youngest members. As you offer petitions for the needs of children, remember to focus on their callings. The following intercessions related to the callings of children may be adapted to fit the particular format, rhythm, and needs of your congregation's worship.

> For children who are called by God, especially those called within situations of great difficulty; for children who suffer from illness, poverty, hunger, homelessness, abuse, or violence.

> For children who call adults to grow in patience, especially for children with special needs, that all of us might accept the invitation of the youngest among us to slow down and serve others.

> For the gifts of laughter, wonder, and imagination that children bring to the world.

> For children who struggle to hear God's voice at home because of neglect or abuse, that other adults will nurture their callings and help them flourish.

> For the children gathered with us today, and all the children in our lives, that our community will welcome their gifts, energy, and enthusiasm.

POEMS TO SPEAK TO THE CALLINGS OF CHILDREN

Three Choices

> For any one problem
> three choices are clear—
>
> Make it worse.
> Make it better.
> Leave it the same.
>
> Again and again
> we are faced with
> these three.
>
> Learning to live
> is like playing
> a game.[1]

—AMY LUDWIG VANDERWATER

Changing

> A ball of yarn becomes a scarf.
> A pup becomes a dog.
> A bowl of cherries turns to pie.
> A tree becomes a log.
>
> A log becomes a rocking chair.
> Mud turns into stone.
> An acorn grows into a tree.
> A body fades to bone.

---

1. VanDerwater, "Three Choices."

Summer bows to winter.
An egg becomes a snake.
A stranger once is now a friend.
Ice becomes a lake.

A giggle grows into a laugh.
Weak turns into strong.
A house becomes a cozy home.
An old dream turns to song.

A pile of twigs becomes a nest.
A thought becomes a book.
Our world is changing every day.
Everywhere you look.[2]

—AMY LUDWIG VANDERWATER

HYMNS TO CELEBRATE THE CALLINGS OF CHILDREN

Christ, Protector of the Children

Lord, we pray you, save all children
    from abuse, disease, despair.
May they grow by love surrounded,
    held within your boundless care.

Give to parents wisdom, patience,
    courage in their testing role;
guide those offering help and counsel,
    making broken families whole.

2. VanDerwater, "Changing."

Christ, you suffered with the suffering,
      felt their sorrow, healed their pain;
your compassion is our model;
      bless our work, our strength sustain.

May we, in our various callings,
      be alert to children's need,
open doors of hope and safety,
      seek the lost, the hungry feed.

Bring back smiles to frightened faces;
      give to fragile bodies health;
may the joy of happy children
      be of greater gain than wealth.

Christ, protector of the children,
      liberator, teacher, friend,
keep us watchful, wise, supportive—
      children's lives on us depend.[3]

SUGGESTED TUNE: STUTTGART (8.7.8.7)

God of Generations

God of generations, we are all your children;
To your church we bring our gifts, our worship and our song.
Young and old we follow, hand in hand together:
In your great love, together we are strong.

Christ, you welcomed children, called us to be like them,
And received a boy's small gift to feed a hungry crowd.
In our church's children, may we see you working:
More than "our future"! They are faithful now.

3. Marshall, "Christ, Protector of the Children."

Part 1: Ages and Stages

Spirit, freely moving, giving youth a vision,
By your grace young Jeremiah heard your loving call;
Mary was a young one when she learned her mission:
Through faithful youth, you offer truth to all.

God of men and women, Helper on our journey,
You have called us in our faith to grow and to mature.
May we keep on learning, worshiping and praying,
That each new day, we'll serve you all the more.

Abraham and Sarah trusted in your promise:
Age was no condition when you gave them work to do.
Old and young we follow, hand in hand together;
At every age, Lord, we belong to you.[4]

SUGGESTED TUNE: NICAEA (12.12.12.10)

---

4. Gillette, "God of Generations."

2

Prayers for Adolescence

GIVEN THE RIGHT CARE and circumstances, adolescents' sense of calling can bloom and ripen. Like children, adolescents do not have "almost vocations," waiting for what or whom they will become as adults. Instead, God calls young people as they are, with roles to play in the church and the wider community. As teens leave childhood behind, they awaken to new joys and possibilities. Adolescents bring gifts to share for the common good: passion and energy, loyalty to friendships and causes, prophetic voices and hearts hungry for justice. Church communities that connect the gifts of teens to the needs of the church can find their communal sense of purpose and mission reenergized in turn, as they show young people a vision of a meaningful life beyond what the dominant culture offers.

Vocation develops in adolescence in four main ways. First, teens can explore particular vocational interests related to work and relationships. Second, adolescents gain and grow into new responsibilities in their families, schools, and community. Third, they begin to make decisions that will have a significant impact on their future. Fourth, teens call forth the vocations of their elders, especially parents and grandparents. When the young Jesus stayed behind in the temple, surprising relatives and strangers alike with his teaching and questions, he claimed his vocation to do the work of the One who

sent him: "Did you not know that I must be in my Father's house?"
(Luke 2:49). Even vocational struggles can allow young people to
grow as Jesus did, "in wisdom and in years" (Luke 2:52).

BLESSINGS FOR MOMENTS AND MILESTONES

A General Blessing for the Callings of Youth

The following blessing may be used when the Sunday Scriptures
include stories of young people called by God, or when stories of
teenagers are featured prominently in the news, whether positively
or negatively.

> Almighty God, again and again
> you have called upon young people
> to force change or fire human hopes.
> Never let older people be so set in their ways
> that they refuse to hear young voices,
> or so firm in their grip on power
> that they reject youth's contributions.
> Let the young be candid, but not cruel.
> Keep them dreaming dreams that you approve,
> and living in the Spirit of the young man Jesus,
> the crucified one who now rules the world. Amen.[1]

A Prayer for a Big Decision

As teens navigate new responsibilities and relationships—starting
to drive, beginning to date, or taking on first jobs—they encounter
unexpected challenges and hard choices. The question *What do
you want to be when you grow up?* also begins to weigh heavily in
adolescence. This prayer for discernment can be offered for teens
who are facing big decisions, prayed by teens themselves, or shared
with parents who want to help guide their teenage children.

1. Presbyterian Church (USA), *Book of Common Worship*, 825.

God of courage,
Guide *N.* as she faces the decision before *her.*
Strengthen *her* faith
and sharpen *her* sight
to see with greater clarity
where you are calling *her* to go
and how you are calling *her* to act.

Give *N.* the courage
to give *herself* to what matters most.
Help *her* to hear your voice
among all the voices competing for *her* attention.
Bless *her* with companions and guides
who will help *her* make wise choices.

Awaken *N.* to your call for *her* life
as *she* seeks to walk in your way.
Open *her* heart to follow your word
and help *her* grow in wisdom
with each new day.

A Blessing for the New School Year for Junior High and High School Students

The beginning of each new school year offers an opportunity to ask God's blessing upon all those involved in the education of youth. This prayer for the start of a new school year invites students, parents, educators, and administrators to pause and consider the tasks of teaching and learning as holy work. You may choose to pray the following litany within worship, invite youth to lead the prayer themselves, or share the blessing with youth ministers as they begin a new year of ministry.

God of Goodness,
    Bless the new school year that lies before us.

You are Alpha and Omega.

>Bless the firsts and lasts that this year will bring.

You are Wisdom and Life.

>Bless the lessons we will learn and the ways we will grow.

You are Truth and Light.

>Bless our study of the past and our work toward the future.

You are Teacher and Guide.

>Bless our teachers and administrators, our parents and coaches.

You are Healer and Reconciler.

>Bless our friends and enemies, our relationships and conflicts.

You are Rock and Refuge.

>Bless our homes and our families, our schools and our communities.

You are Caller and Companion.

>Bless the decisions we will make and the struggles we will face.

You are Creator and Spirit.

>Bless our changes and challenges, our questions and dreams.

In all things, in your name,
Amen.

A Blessing for New Drivers

Teens who earn the right to drive take on a serious responsibility: learning what it means to have someone else's life in their hands. The milestone of earning a driver's license brings both freedom and risk, making it an opportunity to bless youth as they grow into the opportunities and obligations of their callings. You may wish to offer an annual blessing of the keys or driver's licenses of new drivers as a symbol of the community's recognition that youth are growing into the privileges of adulthood.

> O God, yours is the beginning and the ending of our journey:
>
> We thank you for these youth and all that has brought *them* to this moment.
>
> We thank you for
>
> *their* keen sense of adventure,
>
> *their* confidence, and
>
> *their* willingness to take the risks that go with learning to be among us as adults.
>
> We thank you for all that makes *them* and us ready for *them* to be drivers.
>
> Be with *them* in all the times of *their* venturing into life;
>
> Always be alert in *them* to what lies ahead, behind, and beside;
>
> continually enjoying the ride and attentive to the destination;
>
> and bring *them* at last to everlasting life,
>
> through Jesus Christ. Amen.[2]

A Blessing for the End of the School Year

Summer vacation is its own time of transition—an in-between space that mirrors adolescence, caught between the desire for autonomy and the reality of dependence. Blessing the end of the school year and the beginning of the summer season can help both teens and adults approach this season with openness, not trepidation. You could invite a parent and child to read this prayer together within worship.

> God of all times and seasons,
>
> we give you thanks for the year we have shared:
>
> for the lessons we have learned,
>
> for the ways we have grown,
>
> for the wisdom we have gained

2. Benedict, "Rite of Passage."

about ourselves, our world,
and above all, you.

Thank you for the summer that now stretches before us,
inviting us into new rhythms and experiences.
Guide our work and service,
our travel and leisure,
our activities and rest—
so that each day might be blessed by your presence.

As we strive with our families
to balance work and play,
shifting schedules
and changing responsibilities,
grant us your grace and peace.
Let our hearts be open
to receive each other's gifts.
Let our lives make space for each other,
offering love and forgiveness in abundance.
We ask all this in Christ's name.
Amen.

A Blessing for High School Graduation

Graduation from high school marks a watershed moment in the transition from childhood to young adulthood. It can be a time of sadness at leaving childhood friends, the family home, and a familiar community. It is also a time of celebration for a new phase of life to begin. The following blessing could be prayed for an individual or with a group of junior high or high school graduates.

In every beginning is an ending, O Lord,
and in every end something new begins.
Our *brother, N.,* has graduated from high school,
and is ready now for new learning and experiences.

Grant that childhood's innocence and hope may remain alive in *him*,

bringing joy as *he* matures.

Grant that *he* may hear your still small voice in *his* heart saying,

"This is the way; walk in it."

Help *him* preserve old friendships while creating new ones.

Grant that we who love *him* may help *him*

to find *his* own voice, *his* own words, and *his* own word in Christ's true way,

who knows the person *he* was created to be;

we pray this in Jesus's name. *Amen.*[3]

Prayers for Life after Graduation

One way to celebrate the transition from adolescence to adulthood is to bless the work, study, or service that will come after high school. Whether teens pursue a college degree or enter the workforce directly, the following prayers offer ways to call each young person by name and bless the next stage of life as part of their response to God's call.

A Blessing for Beginning College

Gracious God,

your Holy Spirit instructs our hearts in the way of life.

In going to college, your child N. has set aside

a time of learning and preparation for *her* life's work.

Through all the years ahead,

make *her* hungry for wisdom tempered with love.

Help *her* discern the truth in all that *she* learns,

in the people *she* meets,

and in the choices *she* must face each day.

3. Episcopal Church, *Changes*, 22.

Keep *her* mind alert for the rigors of study and exams.

Keep *her* body safe and well.

Give *her* a heart bold to question, yet alive to your wonders.

And assure *her* of your love and ours;

through Christ, your Wisdom made flesh. Amen.[4]

A Blessing for Joining the Workforce

Holy God,

you call us to work as friends of Jesus,

who was sent among us to serve and reconcile.

As *N.* enters the workforce, bless *him* with wisdom and skill.

May the work of *his* hands bring *him* satisfaction.

May *he* be faithful, honest, and fair

with all who labor beside *him,*

and may they be so with *him.*

In all that *he* does, may *he* glorify Christ,

whose saving work on the cross brings us to rest in your love,

and through whom we pray. Amen.[5]

PRAYERS FOR TIMES AND PLACES OF WELCOME

A Prayer for Confirmation Preparation

Confirmation offers an important moment to bless young people's gifts and support their commitment to their faith. Preparation for confirmation can be framed in terms of vocation: an intentional time to discern how God is calling each young person. While denominations have their own rituals and prayers for celebrating confirmation, this blessing for youth can be prayed at the beginning of confirmation classes or within worship.

4. Ibid.
5. Ibid.

God of our callings,
You called the first disciples to follow you.
You call us still today
to grow in wisdom of your ways
and understanding of our faith.
Like the first disciples,
we are called by name,
[as N., N., and N.],
we are blessed with gifts,
and we are sent to serve.
Strengthen our faith in you,
and deepen our commitment
to live as your followers
in the world today.
May your Spirit set our hearts on fire;
may your Son walk with us;
and may your love always guide us.
Amen.

A Prayer for Youth Retreats or Church Camps

Youth retreats and church camps are two popular youth ministry offerings that can provide meaningful and memorable faith encounters for teenagers. Retreats and camps create safe spaces to explore who they are, what they are called to do, and how they are called to serve. Encountering God in nature invites teens to consider their place in the world from a fresh perspective. You may wish to offer this blessing as a group leaves for camp or begins their time of retreat.

Gracious God,
We thank you for this new day
and for all the opportunities you place before us to grow in faith.
We ask your blessing on those who are getting ready to go off to
    camp,

that they may grow in knowledge
and the understanding of your love and grace.
May they be kept safely in your hand.
May they encounter you
in both the beauty of your creation
and in the eyes of their neighbor.
May they feel your presence with them while they are away.
And may they return safely to their homes
better equipped to serve you with the whole of their lives.
In the name of our Savior and Lord, Jesus the Christ.
Amen.[6]

A Prayer for Youth Going on Mission Trips

Mission trips provide a fertile opportunity for engaging youth in their call to service and justice. The following prayer serves to remind the whole community how compassion stands at the heart of their shared Christian calling.

Holy One,
you led your people, night and day, by fire and cloud,
so lead *N. (N., N.,)* by the light of your love.
Go before *him* to prepare a safe path.
Stay beside *him* to instill purpose and joy in *his* mission.
Follow after *him* to leave peace in the wake of wherever *he* has stayed.
Give your angels charge over *his* journey.
At *his* returning, may all *he* has seen be engraved on *his* heart,
and *his* sense of home enlarged forever;
through Jesus Christ, our Savior and Guide. Amen.[7]

---

6. Lutherans Outdoors in South Dakota, "Camp Blessing."
7. Episcopal Church, *Changes*, 23.

PETITIONS FOR THE CALLINGS OF ADOLESCENTS

Teenagers' callings are affirmed when they are included in the cares and concerns of their community. Remembering the gifts and needs of adolescents within the prayers of the people can also encourage older adults to see teenagers as valued members of the congregation.

For our church, that it might be a welcoming place for young men and women—their gifts, perspectives, and questions.

For adults to hear the prophetic voices of youth, and for youth to hear the wisdom of adults.

For all who nurture and support young people on their journeys: parents, grandparents, family, friends, teachers, coaches, employers, and mentors.

For teenagers wrestling with difficult decisions, that they might listen for the still, small voice of God calling in their lives.

For students taking standardized tests and college entrance exams, that they might know that their deepest value lies in being created and loved by God.

For the strength and courage of young people facing challenges at home or school; for victims of injustice and discrimination; for youth who are bullied or who struggle with substance abuse or addiction.

For young people who are challenged to hear God's call in the face of abuse, neglect, violence, poverty, or homelessness.

For the service of young people to our church and the wider community.

POEMS TO SPEAK TO ADOLESCENTS

Start Close In

> *Start close in,*
> *don't take the second step*
> *or the third,*
> *start with the first*
> *thing*
> *close in,*
> *the step*
> *you don't want to take.*

> Start with
> the ground
> you know,
> the pale ground
> beneath your feet,
> your own
> way to begin
> the conversation.

> Start with your own
> question,
> give up on other
> people's questions,
> don't let them
> smother something
> simple.

> To find
> another's voice,
> follow
> your own voice,
> wait until
> that voice

becomes a
private ear
that can
really listen
to another.

Start right now
take a small step
you can call your own
don't follow
someone else's

heroics, be humble
and focused,
start close in,
don't mistake
that other
for your own.

Start close in,
don't take
the second step
or the third,
start with the first
thing
close in,
the step
you don't want to take.[8]

—DAVID WHYTE

8. Whyte, "Start Close In," 360–61.

The Journey

One day you finally knew
what you had to do, and began,
though the voices around you
kept shouting
their bad advice—
though the whole house
began to tremble
and you felt the old tug
at your ankles.
"Mend my life!"
each voice cried.
But you didn't stop.
You knew what you had to do,
though the wind pried
with its stiff fingers
at the very foundations—
though their melancholy
was terrible.
It was already late
enough, and a wild night,
and the road full of fallen
branches and stones.
But little by little,
as you left their voices behind,
the stars began to burn
through the sheets of clouds,
and there was a new voice,
which you slowly
recognized as your own,
that kept you company
as you strode deeper and deeper
into the world,

determined to do
the only thing you could do—
determined to save
the only life you could save.[9]

—MARY OLIVER

HYMNS TO CELEBRATE THE CALLING OF ADOLESCENTS

There Are Many Ways of Sharing

There are many ways of sharing, But God's Spirit gives each one.
There are different ways of caring; It's one Lord whose work is done.
God, whose gifts are overflowing, May we hear you when you call;
Keep us serving, keep us growing, For the common good of all.

We've been baptized in the waters! We've been given work to do.
When you call your sons and daughters, You give gifts for serving
    you.
God, we join in celebration Of the talents you impart.
Bless each baptized one's vocation; Give each one a servant's heart.

All are blest by gifts you give us; Some are set apart to lead.
Give us Jesus' love within us As we care for those in need.
Give us faith to make decisions; Give us joy to share your Word.
Give us unity and vision As we serve your church and world.[10]

SUGGESTED TUNE: NETTLETON (8.7.8.7)

9. Oliver, "The Journey," 38–39.
10. Gillette, "There Are Many Ways of Sharing."

Part 1: Ages and Stages

We Are Called

1. Come! live in the light!
Shine with the joy and the love of the Lord!
We are called to be light for the kingdom,
to live in the freedom of the city of God!

Refrain:
We are called to act with justice.
We are called to love tenderly.
We are called to serve one another, to walk humbly with God.

2. Come! Open your heart!
Show your mercy to all those in fear!
We are called to be hope for the hopeless,
so all hatred and blindness will be no more!

3. Sing! Sing a new song!
Sing of that great day when all will be one!
God will reign and we'll walk with each other as sisters
and brothers united in love![11]

Anthem

Refrain:
We are called, we are chosen.
We are Christ for one another.
We are promised to tomorrow,
while we are for him today.
We are sign, we are wonder.
We are sower, we are seed.
We are harvest, we are hunger.
We are question, we are creed.

11. Haas, "We Are Called," hymn 518.

1. Then where can we stand justified?
In what can we believe?
In no one else but he who suffered,
nothing more than he who rose.
Who was justice for the poor.
Who was rage against the night.
Who was hope for peaceful people.
Who was light.

2. Then how are we to stand at all,
this world of bended knee?
In nothing more than barren shadows.
No one else but he could save us.
Who was justice for the poor.
Who was rage against the night.
Who was hope for peaceful people.
Who was light.

3. Then shall we not stand empty
at the altar of our dreams:
When he promised us ourselves.
Who mark time against tomorrow.
Who are justice for the poor.
Who are rage against the night.
Who are hope for peaceful people.
Who are light.[12]

12. Conry, "Anthem," hymn 494.

3

Prayers for Young Adulthood

YOUNG ADULTHOOD IS A phase of intense vocational searching. Questions of identity, meaning, and purpose press with urgency— and they are questions of calling. Who am I? What I will do in the world? Who will share this life with me? Young adults in their twenties and thirties are making decisions about work, relationships, priorities, and values that will shape their future in permanent ways. They are taking on increasing commitments and responsibilities, both professional and personal. Yet young adulthood still offers enough fluidity and freedom to lend a spirit of possibility and potential to this time in life.

Identifying your community's young adults and learning what vocational questions they are asking is the first step in supporting their callings. Young adulthood embraces a variety of contexts and circumstances: college students, single people, partnered couples (engaged, married, or living together), young families, recent veterans, and new graduates joining the workforce. In recent decades, churches have grown concerned about the declining participation of young adults in congregational life. While changes in religious affiliation have affected institutions and local communities, young adults are not entirely absent from churches either—and they often retain religious identity and spiritual practices beyond formal membership that continue to shape their sense of calling.

Young adulthood tends to involve four primary vocational tasks: completing formal education (whether after high school, college, technical or graduate school), taking on a particular kind of work, discerning relationship commitments (including marriage and parenting), and moving into economic independence. If your community hopes to welcome younger adults—as many congregations do today—engaging their questions of calling is a perfect place to start.

BLESSINGS FOR MOMENTS AND MILESTONES

A General Blessing for the Callings of Young Adults

This blessing for the questions and concerns of young adults can be prayed within worship, at young adult gatherings, or on Sundays that include Scripture stories of young leaders (for example, the call stories of the first disciples or the Pentecost season that celebrates the young adulthood of the early church).

Holy Creator God,

We come before you with hearts, arms, and ears wide open to you.
Out of chaos and darkness you spoke words which brought our
    very being into life.
Although there are so many times that our lives feel chaotic
we remember to listen to the still small voice calling us home to you.

In this world where so many are lost
remind us that your Word is our foundation.
In this world where power is widely abused
remind us of your strength to work for justice.
In this world where the powerful voices of violence are so loud
remind us of your quiet strong voice of peace.

Holy One—give strength to our young adults today
as they pursue and explore your will for them *[us]* in this world.

In the confusing times when we strike out on our own
remind us that you're always there, loving us and holding us close.
Give us the strength to tell our stories of hope, love, and strength
in a world that so desperately needs to hear our voice.

Let us be the models of your Spirit in this life.
In your Holy Name.
Amen![1]

A Blessing for Discernment

Prayers of discernment are valuable spiritual practices for young adults facing significant decisions. Thomas Merton's famous prayer (often used on retreats or in spiritual direction) resonates deeply with young people's yearning, wandering, struggles, and confusion.

> My Lord God, I have no idea where I am going. I do not see the road ahead of me. I cannot know for certain where it will end. Nor do I really know myself, and the fact that I think I am following your will does not mean that I am actually doing so. But I believe that the desire to please you does in fact please you. And I hope I have that desire in all that I am doing. I hope that I will never do anything apart from that desire. And I know that if I do this, you will lead me by the right road, though I may know nothing about it. Therefore I will trust you always though I may seem to be lost and in the shadow of death. I will not fear, for you are ever with me, and you will never leave me to face my perils alone.[2]

A Blessing at College Graduation

Finishing formal education is a major milestone in young adulthood. As with most vocational transitions, graduation from technical school, college, or graduate school can bring conflicting

1. Sexton, "Prayer for Worship."
2. Merton, *Thoughts in Solitude*, 79.

emotions: joy at what has been completed, sadness at what will be left behind, anxiety about the unknown, and excitement about what lies ahead. Consider using this turning point to bless the young people in your midst and promise prayerful support as they move forward. This prayer may be prayed as a sending forth at the end of worship or prayed by parents or grandparents for the graduates in their families.

> May God, who is present in sunrise and nightfall
> and in the crossing of the sea,
> guide your feet as you go.
>
> May God, who is with you when you sit
> and when you stand,
> encompass you with love
> and lead you by the hand.
>
> May God, who knows your path
> and the places where you rest,
> be with you in your waiting,
> be your good news for sharing,
> and lead you in the way that is everlasting.[3]

A Blessing before Starting a New Job

Work is a primary part of the identity of most young adults. Today's career paths include many more job changes than previous generations have experienced, making it all the more pressing and powerful to bless a young person in the midst of transition. This blessing can be used one on one with a young adult, spoken during worship at the end of the school year (especially in campus ministry), or offered by parents to their young adult children.

> Holy God,

3. Claiborne and Wilson-Hartgrove, *Common Prayer*, 71.

you call us to do the works of Christ
who came to live among us in love as a servant.
Our true call is to be transformed into his likeness.
As *N.* begins this new job,
grant *him* wisdom and skill,
so that the work of *his* hands
may bring *him* satisfaction.
Help *him* to be faithful, honest, and fair
with those who labor beside *him*,
and let them be so with *him*.
May *he* glorify you in all *he* does,
through Christ whose saving work on the cross
brings us to rest in your love.
Amen.[4]

A Prayer for Moving from the Family Home

Whenever the moment of leaving the family home arrives, the emotional transition creates a ripple effect that changes the callings of all involved: parents, children, siblings, and other companions. Depending on the size of your community, you could offer this prayer within worship or share it with a family to bless its own members on this milestone in young adulthood.

Your Spirit, O God,
keeps us moving ever forward in faith
as you call us to new places and new beginnings.
Your servant *N.* is leaving the home of *her* childhood
to a home of *her* own.
We give thanks for *her* newfound independence
and the courage to care for *herself.*
May the place *she* is leaving withstand *her* loss.
May the home *she* is creating

---

4. Episcopal Church, *Changes*, 43.

become a place of shelter and peace.
And may we all come to know
our true and eternal home in your heart;
through Christ our Lord.
Amen.[5]

A Blessing for Those Who Are Single

Since young adults today tend to delay marriage and parenthood, single life has become a longer and more defining experience of young adulthood than in previous generations. Some young adults go on to commit to spouses or partners; others discover that being single is their life's commitment. Blessing the callings of those who are single is an important sign that your community believes each person is called by God as they are today, not simply as being on the way to something else.

> Gracious God, none who trust in your Son can be separated from your love. Give to those who live alone peace and contentment in their solitude, hope and fulfillment in their love of you, and joy and companionship in their relations with others; through Jesus Christ our Lord. Amen.[6]

A Blessing for an Engaged Couple

Engagement is a vocational turning point: a moment of celebration for the couple, their families and friends, but also a joyful occasion for the entire community who will be blessed by their commitment. This prayer for an engaged couple can be offered within worship or during wedding preparation meetings with church staff.

> God of love,

5. Ibid., 23.

6. Evangelical Lutheran Church in America, *Evangelical Lutheran Worship*, 83.

You have called this couple to marriage:
to join their lives together,
to build and share a future.
You have also called them in their engagement:
to look ahead to what comes next
and to grow in love where they are today.

As they plan and prepare
for celebrations that lie ahead,
help them hear your deeper, lasting call
to a new vocation:
a marriage given in love, shared with others, and growing in faith.

We ask your blessing upon this couple,
their families and friends,
and all who will guide and support them on their journey.
May this time of preparation
deepen their faith in you
and their trust in one another.

We ask this in the name of Jesus your Son,
who calls us to love.
Amen.

A Blessing for a Newly Married Couple

Once a couple has celebrated their wedding, their new vocation is only beginning. Blessing a newly married couple invites the whole community to offer their prayers and support. The blessing could also be prayed on a couple's anniversary as they grow into the calling of marriage.

Almighty God, giver of life and love, bless N. and N. Grant them wisdom and devotion in the ordering of their common life, that each may be to the other a strength in need, a counselor in perplexity, a comfort in sorrow, and a companion in joy. And so knit their wills together in your will and their spirits in your Spirit, that they may live together in love and peace all the days of their life; through Jesus Christ our Lord. *Amen.*[7]

A Blessing for New Parents

The transition to parenthood, which often happens in young adulthood, can bring significant upheaval to the multiple callings of new parents. Marking this major life change with prayer extends a loving welcome to a new family during a time when they are in need of a supportive community. The following blessing can speak to biological, adoptive, and foster parenthood and may be used for the arrival of a first child or subsequent children.

> O God, you have taught us through your blessed Son that whoever receives a little child in the name of Christ receives Christ himself: We give you thanks for the blessing you have bestowed upon this family in giving them a child. Confirm their joy by a lively sense of your presence with them, and give them calm strength and patient wisdom as they seek to bring this child to love all that is true and noble, just and pure, lovable and gracious, excellent and admirable, following the example of our Lord and Savior, Jesus Christ. *Amen.*[8]

PRAYERS FOR TIMES AND PLACES OF WELCOME

A Prayer for Young Adult Ministry

Young adults need safe spaces in which to share their stories and questions. They need peers who provide companionship for the journey and mentors who offer wisdom from their own experiences. The following prayer can be prayed by a group during young

7. Episcopal Church, *Book of Common Prayer,* 444.

8. Ibid., 443.

adult ministry gatherings or by mentors meeting with young adults who are wrestling with questions of calling.

Leader: You keep us waiting . . .
you, the God of all time,
want us to wait for the right time
in which to discover
who we are,
where we must go,
who will be with us,
and what we must do.
All: So, thank you . . .
for the waiting time.

Leader: You keep us looking . . .
you, the God of all space,
want us to look in the right and wrong places
for signs of hope,
for people who are hopeless,
for visions of a better world
which will appear among the disappointments
of the world we know.
All: So, thank you . . .
for the looking time.

Leader: You keep us loving . . .
you, the God whose name is love,
want us to be like you—
to love the loveless and the unloved and the unlovely;
to love without jealousy or design or threat;
and most difficult of all,
to love ourselves.
All: So, thank you . . .
for the loving time.

Leader: And in all this,
you keep us . . .
through hard questions with no easy answers;
through failing where we hoped to succeed,
and making an impact
when we thought we were useless;
through the patience and encouragement
and love of others;
and through Jesus Christ and the Holy Spirit,
you keep us.
All: So, thank you . . .
for the keeping time
and for now and for ever.
Amen.[9]

A Prayer for Homecoming

Young adults often return to churches for homecoming occasions like weddings, funerals, baptisms, Christmas, and Easter. Moments of return also come with college students on school break, engaged couples seeking to be married, and young parents bringing children for baptism or religious education. This homecoming prayer can be offered during worship to celebrate the presence of young adults and remind them they are always a part of your community's cares and concerns.

God of loving welcome,

When we are lost and cannot find our way,
you reach out to welcome us home.
When we are grieving and cannot find peace,
you reach out to welcome us home.
When we are searching for guidance and wisdom,
you reach out to welcome us home.

9. Wild Goose Worship Group, *Wee Worship Book*, 57–58.

While we are looking for answers to questions,
you call out, inviting us home.
While we are longing for friends and companions,
you call out, inviting us home.
While we are seeking to know and to trust you,
you call out, inviting us home.

When we return to support one another,
you delight to gather us home.
When we rejoice and celebrate together,
you delight to gather us home.
When we remember your love and your promise,
you delight to gather us home.

Amen.

PETITIONS FOR THE CALLINGS OF YOUNG ADULTS

Through regular petitions offered in worship, a community can speak a hopeful word to young adults' diverse circumstances, challenges, and joys. A faith community that offers a safe, supportive place for searching and discerning provides important welcome and comfort to young adults seeking to grow in faith, too.

> For young people growing in wisdom, and for the persistence to listen for the voice of God amid many other voices clamoring for their attention.
>
> For all who mentor younger generations—for the wisdom of educators and employers to teach, and for the openness of young adults to listen.
>
> For young adults burdened by student loan debt and other financial stresses, that their commitment to their callings may still find ways to flourish.

For young people struggling to hear God's voice in their lives, especially those who suffer from depression, anxiety, or other mental health concerns.

For couples discerning marriage, that they might invite God into their dreaming and planning.

For professionals starting out in their careers and for all those searching for work.

For couples trying to conceive and all those who feel frustrated in their callings.

For young adults in transition: for veterans returning from deployment, for recent graduates, for expectant parents, and for those beginning new work.

For those who are single by choice and for those who are searching for a partner, that our community may welcome their gifts and pray for their needs, no matter where they are on their journey.

POEMS TO SPEAK TO YOUNG ADULTHOOD

Things to Watch Out For

You can pay attention and still trip on tree roots and fall. You can grow
colder. You can be led into the wilderness and lug a pack
of things you don't need. You can lose your way. You can find
yourself sustained. All day you can complain and at night gaze
at a million stars. Both legs can ache. You can hope this is worth it
but doubt it.

You can imagine what everyone at home is doing.
You can be comforted. You can remain inconsolable. Before you go
you can locate the wilderness on a map, drive there, park the car,
stroll in and out in thirty minutes dreaming
of escape routes. You can confuse boundaries and stumble
from one wilderness to the next. You can be tempted

in the wilderness. You can wonder what the point is.
Four minutes can feel like forty years. You can be sure
you cannot carry this much weight for that much longer. Unexpectedly,
a way can be made in the wilderness. A stream can appear
without a bridge. You can cross on a high log, look back
and feel strong. You can weaken. It can rain. Lightning can strike,

a fire start, angels can surprise you. So can snakes and bears.
You can crave pizza and receive manna. You can drop the wine.
You can get into trouble, forget to bring a whistle, shout for help
and no one will answer. Why not give up? You can trust.
You can lack trust. You can nap and hope, stand or kneel.
You can wait. In the wilderness you can hear someone coming.[10]

—MARLENE MULLER

Patient Trust

Above all, trust in the slow work of God.
We are quite naturally impatient in everything
to reach the end without delay.
We would like to skip the intermediate stages.
We are impatient of being on the way
to something unknown, something new.

And yet, it is the law of all progress
that it is made by passing through
some stages of instability—
and that it may take a very long time.

And so I think it is with you;
your ideas mature gradually—let them grow,

10. Muller, "Things to Watch Out For."

let them shape themselves, without undue haste.
Don't try to force them on,
as though you could be today what time
(that is to say, grace and circumstances
acting on your own good will)
will make of you tomorrow.

Only God could say what this new spirit
gradually forming in you will be.
Give our Lord the benefit of believing
that his hand is leading you,
and accept the anxiety of feeling yourself
in suspense and incomplete.[11]

—PIERRE TEILHARD DE CHARDIN, SJ

HYMNS TO CELEBRATE THE CALLINGS OF YOUNG ADULTS

In the Lord I'll Be Ever Thankful

In the Lord I'll be ever thankful,
In the Lord I will rejoice.
Look to God, do not be afraid.
Lift up your voices, the Lord is near.
Lift up your voices, the Lord is near.[12]

Here I Am, Lord

1. I, the Lord of sea and sky,
I have heard my people cry.

11. Teilhard de Chardin, "Patient Trust," 58.
12. Taizé, "In the Lord I'll Be Ever Thankful," hymn 396.

All who dwell in dark and sin
My hand will save.
I, who made the stars of night,
I will make their darkness bright.
Who will bear my light to them?
Whom shall I send?

Refrain:
Here I am, Lord.
Is it I, Lord?
I have heard you calling in the night.
I will go, Lord,
if you lead me.

I will hold your people in my heart.

2. I, the Lord of snow and rain,
I have borne my people's pain.
I have wept for love of them.
They turn away.
I will break their hearts of stone,
Give them hearts for love alone.
I will speak my word to them.
Whom shall I send?

3. I, the Lord of wind and flame,
I will tend the poor and lame.
I will set a feast for them.
My hand will save.
Finest bread I will provide
Till their hearts be satisfied.
I will give my life to them.
Whom shall I send?[13]

13. Schutte, "Here I Am, Lord," hymn 492.

The Summons

1. Will you come and follow me
If I but call your name?
Will you go where you don't know
And never be the same?
Will you let my love be shown,
Will you let my name be known,
Will you let my life be grown
In you and you in me?

2. Will you leave yourself behind
If I but call your name?
Will you care for cruel and kind
And never be the same?
Will you risk the hostile stare
Should your life attract or scare?
Will you let me answer pray'r
In you and you in me?

3. Will you let the blinded see
If I but call your name?
Will you set the pris'ners free
And never be the same?
Will you kiss the leper clean,
And do such as this unseen,
And admit to what I mean
In you and you in me?

4. Will you love the "you" you hide
If I but call your name?
Will you quell the fear inside
And never be the same?
Will you use the faith you've found
To reshape the world around,

Through my sight and touch and sound
In you and you in me?

5. Lord, your summons echoes true
When you but call my name.
Let me turn and follow you
And never be the same.
In your company I'll go
Where your love and footsteps show.
Thus I'll move and live and grow
In you and you in me.[14]

14. Bell, "Summons," hymn 510.

4

Prayers for Middle Adulthood

MIDDLE ADULTHOOD IS THE longest phase of adult life, made up of decades of the daily living out of vocation. Adults in the "prime of life" need supportive communities for the long haul of their vocations: building careers, raising children, and serving in the community. This can be a time of spiritual grounding—coming to terms with the reality that "life is not all about me" and trying to lead a good life that gives back in return—but also a time of spiritual struggle related to vocational crisis.

The middle years of adulthood involve three main areas of vocational growth: settling into vocational commitments (such as marriage, parenting, or the single life), negotiating multiple callings to work and family, and taking on unexpected callings such as caring for aging relatives or friends. In the middle years of adulthood, people must come to terms with having chosen and made this particular life and not another—or that it has chosen and made them. This acceptance can be a profound experience of finitude and mortality, but can also bring the deepening of humility and the beginning of wisdom.

Middle adulthood is an age full of paradoxes. Middle-aged adults are independent, yet many others depend on them. They have freedom but also great responsibilities. They are full of ideals yet must deal with the realities around them. Middle adulthood is also a time that calls forth sacrifices of time, energy, and passion. This is the time of life when multiple callings press most insistently, especially for those in the "sandwich generation," caring for children as well as aging parents. Middle-aged adults can be called in multiple ways (as spouse or partner, parent, sibling, friend, neighbor, employee or employer, citizen, church member, and community volunteer), yet they often need guidance in claiming these roles and responsibilities as callings. Your congregation can help by finding opportunities to bless the vocations of middle-aged adults, even though the milestones and transitions of middle adulthood are often less obvious or public than those of other stages.

BLESSINGS FOR MOMENTS AND MILESTONES

A General Blessing for the Callings of Midlife

The following blessing may be prayed over adults who are facing vocational questions or embarking on a new endeavor. The metaphor of pilgrimage speaks to the long journey of middle adulthood: a quest for deeper meaning, a winding road through peaks and valleys, a search for steady companions and enduring strength. The prayer may also be fitting for adult education classes or small groups.

> Christ our Guide,
> stay with us on our pilgrimage through life:
> When we falter, encourage us,
> when we stumble, steady us,
> and when we have fallen, pick us up.
> Help us to become, step by step, more truly ourselves,
> and remind us that you have travelled this way before us.
> Amen.[1]

---

1. Ashwin, *Book of a Thousand Prayers*, 69.

A Prayer for Discernment in Adulthood

Vocational questioning does not end once career choices and major life commitments have been made. Middle adulthood is still a time for grappling with important discernments and living into the consequences, navigating daily decisions and life-changing transitions related to callings. While the following blessing for discernment can apply to other ages in the lifespan, its desire for clarity and courage speaks to the particular needs of middle adulthood.

> Lord, let me know clearly
> the work which You are calling me to do in life.
> And grant me every grace I need
> to answer Your call
> with courage and love
> and lasting dedication to Your will.[2]

A Prayer for Stewardship

Middle-aged adults are called to be leaders and stewards: caring for children and aging relatives, tending to their homes and their workplaces, and serving in their communities. Through this work, many adults in midlife also awaken to a realization of their own limits. The following prayer (commonly misattributed to Archbishop Oscar Romero) has become a popular reflection on humility, tempering the desire for success and quick results with the wisdom that each of our vocations is only a part of the purposes of God.

> It helps, now and then, to step back and take the long view.
> The kingdom of God is not only beyond our efforts,
> it is beyond our imagination.
>
> We accomplish in our lifetime only a tiny fraction
> of the magnificent enterprise that is God's work.
> Nothing we do is complete, which is another way of saying
> that the kingdom always lies beyond us.

2. Episcopal Diocese of Alabama, "Vocare Prayer."

No statement says all that could be said.
No prayer fully expresses our faith.
No confession brings perfection.
No pastoral visit brings wholeness.
No program accomplishes the church's mission.
No set of goals and objectives includes everything.

This is what we are about:
We plant seeds that one day will grow.
We water seeds already planted,
knowing that they hold future promise.
We lay foundations that will need further development.
We provide yeast that produces effects beyond our capabilities.

We cannot do everything
And there is a sense of liberation in realizing that.
This enables us to do something, and to do it very well.
It may be incomplete, but it is a beginning,
A step along the way,
An opportunity for God's grace to enter and do the rest.

We may never see the end results, but that is the difference between
The master builder and the worker.
We are workers, not master builders; ministers, not messiahs.
We are prophets of a future not our own.[3]

A Blessing for Family Life

Middle adulthood offers important moments to bless families. More people are marrying or starting to raise children in middle adulthood; others divorce, remarry, or blend families during this stage. Middle-aged adults must consider their spouse, children, or parents when discerning how to live out their own callings. You

3. Untener, "Archbishop Oscar Romero Prayer."

may wish to use this blessing for families (and the adults who lead them) during worship or family gatherings for religious education. The prayer can also be given to families as a daily prayer at home.

> God of compassion,
> whose Son Jesus Christ, the child of Mary,
> shared the life of a home in Nazareth,
> and on the cross drew the whole human family to himself:
> strengthen us in our daily living
> that in joy and in sorrow
> we may know the power of your presence
> to bind together and to heal;
> through Jesus Christ our Lord.
> Amen.[4]

A Blessing for Caregiving

Caregiving is an example of a calling that is given but not asked for. Care for children, youth with special needs, or aging relatives can demand significant time and attention from middle-aged adults. These obligations and duties often require that adults set aside their own desires in order to serve those who need their love and attention. Yet even when a calling feels overwhelming or unwelcome at the beginning, the growing awareness that one is cooperating with the purposes of God can lead to deeper joy or fulfillment. As more and more adults become caregivers, congregations will have increasing opportunities to bless and support this significant—and often overlooked—calling.

> In the circle of life, O Gracious One,
> your signs of love shine out in every situation,
> through dying and rebirth, growing up and growing old, holding on and letting go.
> Now *N., N., and N.,* will be looking after their parent(s), *N., [and N].*

---

4. Archbishops' Council, "Prayer for Family Life."

Those who gave care now need to receive care;
those who once were supported by them need be supporters.
We pray this family may gracefully accept these changes.
Grant them wisdom, good humor, patience and hope,
as life continues according to your constant love,
and bless their days with wellness, safety, and peace;
through Christ our Redeemer. *Amen.*[5]

A Prayer for Work-Life Balance

Work and family responsibilities compete for time and attention in middle adulthood. People often say they are "pulled in many directions," "juggling responsibilities," or "stretched thin." While perfect balance is an elusive myth, the desire for greater integration between multiple callings remains an important spiritual concern. Consider reframing the search for balance as a desire for a life centered in God's purposes. This blessing for middle adulthood can be prayed within worship to affirm the many "dear loves and worthy tasks" that make up vocation in midlife.

Eternal God,
you have led us through our days and years,
made wisdom ripe and faith mature.
Show men and women your purpose for them,
so that, when youth is spent,
they may not find life empty or labor stale,
but may devote themselves
to dear loves and worthy tasks,
with undiminished strength;
for the sake of Jesus Christ the Lord. Amen.[6]

---

5. Episcopal Church, *Changes*, 45.
6. Presbyterian Church (USA), *Book of Common Worship*, 833.

A Blessing after Losing a Job

Callings can end. Changing jobs or careers is common in middle adulthood, as adults often have to learn when and how to take leave of employment situations. In the face of disappointment, disillusionment, or failure related to work, adults in midlife need the support and healing offered by communities of faith. Praying over someone who has lost a job can be a powerful way for your community to demonstrate its care and concern for its members and their daily work. The following prayer also includes an option in brackets to bless the individual's search for new work.

> Author of Life,
> you ordered the seasons and watch over the times
> between sowing and reaping, fallow and planting.
> We pray with *N*., whose work in this place has now ended.
> During *her* years at this job,
> *she* faithfully accomplished *her* tasks,
> befriending those who worked beside *her*.
> Bless *her* as *she* leaves [and enters a period of waiting].
> Bring relief if *she* is anxious.
> Strengthen *her* trust in you [and guide *her* search for new work].
> By the power of the Holy Spirit,
> assure *her* of your continuing love and care,
> and of *her* usefulness in the work of your kingdom;
> through Christ the Worker, our ever present help and companion.
>   Amen.[7]

A Prayer for a New Job

Given the central place of work in adult life, churches that want to engage their members around questions of vocation need to speak to their work: giving thanks for a new position, blessing people when they have to move for a job, or praying for mentors to guide

---

7. Episcopal Church, *Changes*, 43.

those looking to move ahead. The following blessing for work may be prayed over adults graduating from college or other studies, people in career transition, or professionals reentering the workforce after caring for family.

God of beginnings,
you make each day fresh with dawn.
You make smooth the rough places
and make straight our ways through the wilderness.

Today we ask your blessing on N. as *she* begins a new job.
We give thanks for the wisdom and knowledge *she* brings to her work,
all that *she* has gained and learned from what came before.

We praise you for the gift of *her* work,
for the chance to grow and learn
and serve your world.

We pray for a smooth transition
as *she* encounters new people, places, and ways of working.

We ask you to bless *her*
with strength and peace of mind,
with energy and resilience,
with courage and hope.

We surround *her* as a sign of your love
and pledge our support
to walk with her in her work,
today and always.

Amen.

Prayers for a Time of Crisis

Where is God's call in the midst of loss and grief? What does it mean to change course from what seemed to be a clear plan? How can the end of a calling be the beginning of something new and changed? A person's sense of calling can be devastated by crisis, leaving confusion, anger, or bitterness in its wake of churning questions. By praying for those in vocational crisis, your community can care for people in their most broken and vulnerable moments. The following blessings for a time of crisis offer ways to support people in difficulty, both publicly and privately. The first may be prayed in worship or privately with a family or couple; the second may be offered for personal prayer and support.

> God who is with us
> at our beginning and ending,
> be with us now,
> help us to find you
> in the chaos of our lives,
> let your light shine in our darkness
> so that we may be guided
> to walk in your ways, all the days of our lives.[8]

> Lord, I am poured out,
> I come to you for renewal.
> Lord, I am weary,
> I come to you for refreshment.
> Lord, I am worn,
> I come to you for restoration.
> Lord, I am lost,
> I come to you for guidance.
> Lord, I am troubled,
> I come to you for peace.
> Lord, I am lonely,
> I come to you for love.

8. Monberg, "God Who Is With Us," 110.

Come, Lord,
Come revive me
Come re-shape me
Come mould me in your image.
Re-cast me in the furnace of your love.[9]

A Prayer for Those Who Are Separated or Divorced

The complex pain and suffering caused by the end of a calling to marriage are difficult to share publicly. But the power of blessing and supporting those who are in the midst of this struggle cannot be underestimated. The following prayer touches a variety of emotions and experiences related to separation and divorce, gathering them within the embrace of a loving, comforting God who calls people to fullness of life. (Depending on the circumstances of the group, you may wish to add or substitute "divorced" for "separated.")

In prayer we embrace all God's people who, having married,
are now separated—women and men;
those who separated early in their marriage
and those who separated later;
those who feel themselves the victims of separation
and those who blame themselves;
those whose separating was relatively calm,
and those for whom it was a bitter and violent experience.

It is our faith that God graces marriage with an infinite beauty.
But it is also our faith that God's heart grieves
for all who have been disappointed in life.
We believe that God feels with and for all
whose experience didn't match up to their dream.

We too feel God's feelings
and we pray for our sisters and brothers who are separated.

9. Adam, *Power Lines*, 57.

May Jesus, whose touch healed so many and so powerfully
when he walked on earth, touch and heal you.

Where you feel a failure, may he ease your recrimination;
Where you feel disappointment, may he reassure your spirit;
Where you feel resentful, may he help any evil in your heart to die;
Where you feel victimized, may he be your vindication;
Where you feel guilty, may he rejoice in your repentance.

We especially pray for a bright future for separated people,
lest they be imprisoned in memories of pain.
We pray that they rediscover love.
May all who have been disappointed by marriage
find again the vocation to love and the experience of love
that is at the heart of being human for all of us.[10]

PRAYERS FOR TIMES AND PLACES OF WELCOME

Prayers for Church Committees

Middle adulthood is often when adults move into congregational leadership roles. Ideally this involvement is part of each person's calling, drawing forth their particular gifts to serve the community. Blessing the call to work in religious education, worship, or other church committees affirms this service as part of the Christian calling. The following prayers can be used by congregational groups and led by lay members as well as ministers.

> Almighty God, your Holy Spirit equips the church with a rich variety of gifts. Grant that we may use them to bear witness to Christ in lives that are built on faith and love. Make us ready to live the gospel and eager to do your will, so that we may share with all your church in the joys of eternal life; through Jesus Christ, our Savior and Lord.[11]

10. Harrington, *Prayer Reflections*, 67.
11. Evangelical Lutheran Church in America, *Pastoral Care*, 392.

Almighty God, you have called us to labor in your vineyard, and without you we can do nothing. Grant your gracious presence at this meeting, that what we do will build up your whole church. Let your Holy Spirit govern and direct us, that we may consult together peacefully, pleasing you with all that we say and do; through Jesus Christ, our Savior and Lord.[12]

PETITIONS FOR THE CALLINGS OF MIDLIFE

While middle adulthood can be seen as the most powerful and productive of all the lifespan stages, it can also be isolating when people lack adequate support or life-giving work. Middle-aged adults need a community's prayerful support to help them steward the people, places, resources, and dreams to which they have been called.

For all those dealing with unemployment or underemployment, that they may find the work to which they are called.

For all who feel pulled between work and home, responsibilities and relationships, and those who desire greater peace between their multiple callings.

For the joys of family life—for laughter, love, and growth together.

For single parents; for parents working to raise their children together after divorce; for stepparents caring for blended families.

For individuals and families dealing with alcoholism or addiction, and for the courage of communities that support them.

For couples dealing with infertility, miscarriage, stillbirth, or a difficult prenatal diagnosis.

For those who give care and those who receive care, especially for adult children caring for their parents.

For couples struggling in their marriage and for couples facing separation or divorce.

For the joys of work: for clients served, patients helped, students taught, and projects done well.

For support between coworkers, for respect between employers and employees, and for the guidance of mentors and those they nurture.

12. Ibid., 391.

For adults in the midst of transition, whether a geographic move, a new job, a return to school, or a change in an important relationship.

POEMS TO SPEAK TO ADULTHOOD IN MIDLIFE

Excerpt from "The Farm"

Be thankful and repay
Growth with good work and care.
Work done in gratitude,
Kindly, and well, is prayer.
You did not make yourself,
Yet you must keep yourself
By use of other lives.
No gratitude atones
For bad use or too much.

This is not work for hire.
By this expenditure
You make yourself a place;
You make yourself a way
For love to reach the ground.
In its ambition and
Its greed, its violence,
The world is turned against
This possibility,
And yet the world survives
By the survival of
This kindly working love.[13]

—WENDELL BERRY

13. Berry, "Farm," 141.

How Good to Center Down!

How good it is to center down!

To sit quietly and see one's self pass by!

The streets of our minds seethe with endless traffic;

Our spirits resound with clashings, with noisy silences,

While something deep within hungers and thirsts for the still moment and the resting lull.

With full intensity we seek, ere the quiet passes, a fresh sense of order in our living;

A direction, a strong sure purpose that will structure our confusion and bring meaning in our chaos.

We look at ourselves in this waiting moment—the kinds of people we are.

The questions persist: what are we doing with our lives?—what are the motives that order our days?

What is the end of our doings? Where are we trying to go?

Where do we put the emphasis and where are our values focused?

For what end do we make sacrifices? Where is my treasure and what do I love most in life?

What do I hate most in life and to what am I true?

Over and over the questions beat in upon the waiting moment.

As we listen, floating up through all the jangling echoes of our turbulence, there is a sound of another kind—

A deeper note which only the stillness of the heart makes clear.

It moves directly to the core of our being. Our questions are answered,

Our spirits refreshed, and we move back into the traffic of our daily round

With the peace of the Eternal in our step.

How good it is to center down![14]

—HOWARD THURMAN

14. Thurman, "How Good to Center Down!" 28–29.

HYMNS TO CELEBRATE MIDDLE ADULTHOOD

Lord of All Hopefulness

1. Lord of all hopefulness, Lord of all joy,
Whose trust, ever childlike, no cares can destroy,
Be there at our waking, and give us, we pray,
Your bliss in our hearts, Lord, at the break of the day.

2. Lord of all eagerness, Lord of all faith,
Whose strong hands were skilled at the plane and the lathe,
Be there at our labors, and give us, we pray,
Your strength in our hearts, Lord, at the noon of the day.

3. Lord of all kindliness, Lord of all grace,
Your hands swift to welcome, your arms to embrace,
Be there at our homing, and give us, we pray,
Your love in our hearts, Lord, at the eve of the day.

4. Lord of all gentleness, Lord of all calm,
Whose voice is contentment, whose presence is balm,
Be there at our sleeping, and give us, we pray,
Your peace in our hearts, Lord, at the end of the day.[15]

SUGGESTED TUNE: SLANE (10.10.10.10)

The Servant Song

1. Will you let me be your servant,
Let me be as Christ to you;
Pray that I might have the grace to
Let you be my servant, too.

15. Struther, "Lord of All Hopefulness," hymn 568.

2. We are pilgrims on a journey,
We are trav'lers on the road;
We are here to help each other
Walk the mile and bear the load.

3. I will hold the Christ-light for you
In the night-time of your fear;
I will hold my hand out to you,
Speak the peace you long to hear.

4. I will weep when you are weeping;
When you laugh, I'll laugh with you.
I will share your joy and sorrow
'Til we've seen this journey through.

5. When we sing to God in heaven
We shall find such harmony,
Born to all we've known together
Of Christ's love and agony.

6. Will you let me be your servant,
Let me be as Christ to you;
Pray that I might have the grace to
Let you be my servant, too.[16]

16. Gillard, "Servant Song," hymn 476.

5

Prayers for Later Adulthood

LATER ADULTHOOD IS A long turning. It is a time of continuity with midlife but also a time of change with its own vocational questions. This stage brings the end of certain callings (like paid professional work) and the beginning of other callings (such as grandparenting). Later adulthood can be a time of generativity as people reach the end of their professional careers. They continue to serve as leaders, concerned with the well-being of their workplaces, families, and communities, but they are also looking toward the next stage of life.

Later adulthood tends to affect vocation in four main areas. It brings shifting patterns of work and service. It invites renewed discernment about identity and purpose. It responds to losses in relationships or physical ability. It explores how to integrate core values and beliefs into one's legacy and future. Later adulthood brings many transitions: retirement, "empty nesting," downsizing, or moving. It can be a joyful season of harvesting the fruits of one's labors. It can also be a struggle of accepting changes and realizing new limitations. Yet there remains an abiding call from God that endures through transitions and offers comfort for uncertainty about what lies ahead.

BLESSINGS FOR MOMENTS AND MILESTONES

A General Blessing for the Callings of Later Adulthood

This blessing for later adulthood may be offered when the Sunday Scripture readings speak of adults making changes later in life (for example, Abraham and Sarah) or when you wish to honor the presence and service of adults within your community.

> O God,
> you have called your servants
> to ventures of which we cannot see the ending,
> by paths as yet untrodden,
> through perils unknown.
> Give us faith to go out with good courage,
> not knowing where we go,
> but only that your hand is leading us
> and your love supporting us;
> through Jesus Christ our Lord. Amen.[1]

A Prayer for Discernment

Popular culture often paints the later decades of adulthood as a time of wisdom. While introspection, reconciliation, and acceptance can be fruits of later adulthood, it can also be a time when unsettling questions arise about identity, meaning, and purpose—existential questions at the heart of vocation. The following blessing for discernment speaks to both personal and professional situations in later adulthood. The communal tone of the prayer invites the whole congregation to remember that discernment is a lifelong call.

> Grant us a vision, Lord
> To see what we can achieve
> To reach out beyond ourselves

1. Topping, *Daily Prayer*, 85.

To share our lives with others
To stretch our capabilities
To increase our sense of purpose
To be aware of where we can help
To be sensitive to your Presence
To give heed to your constant call.[2]

A Prayer in Time of Change

Later adulthood is characterized by shifts in how time and the body are experienced. After midlife, adults often realize that more years are now behind them than ahead of them. Time begins to feel as if it is passing faster and is fleeting. The body is changing, whether gradually or suddenly. This stage of life raises questions of how to live into the coming decades when the world—and one's own body, which inhabits it—seems to be changing so quickly. This blessing for a time of change offers a prayer for courage and faith in God's guidance.

O God,
you call us from our settled ways,
out of old habits and rutted traditions.
You call us into the land of promise,
to new life and new possibilities.
Make us strong to travel the road ahead.
Deliver us from false security and comfort,
desire for ease and uninvolved days.
Let your Word and Spirit dwell in us
That your will may be fulfilled in us
For the well-being and shalom of all.
In the name of Jesus Christ, we pray.
Amen.[3]

2. Adam, *Power Lines*, 45.
3. Anderson, *Prayers of our Hearts*, 59.

A Blessing for Retirement

Vocation does not end with retirement. Yet this change affects identity and well-being in significant and sometimes surprising ways. Retirees often need to reconstruct a sense of meaning and purpose through new roles or relationships in order to continue using their gifts in service of the common good. In a culture void of meaningful rites of passage for taking leave of paid work, congregations that honor the life transition of retirement through religious rituals help bridge the gap. The following blessing can be prayed over the person retiring and their family (since retirement brings changes for both partners in a couple and for the extended family). Consider inviting the individual being honored to participate in worship in a special way; for example, reading the prayers of the people.

> To everything, Lord, you have given a season,
> calling each thing good in its time.
> In the years of our lives,
> you call us to work,
> you ask us to play,
> you command us to rest,
> and by your grace, you weave our days together in peace.
> We pray for our *brother N.*, who comes to the end of *his* season of work.
> Thank you for friends made, challenges met, and growth enjoyed,
> and for all *he* has learned and accomplished.
> Help *him* now let the old work go,
> to take up the new life for which you have also given *him* gifts;
> through Christ the Worker, in whose love is our eternal rest and joy.
> Amen.[4]

---

4. Episcopal Church, *Changes*, 53.

A Blessing for an Empty Nest

Later adulthood often brings changes to families, as children move out and make their own way in the world and parents adjust to the new dynamic. This shift illustrates the interdependence of callings and how our identity and purpose is connected with those we love. A child leaving the family home provides an opportunity to bless the whole family and acknowledge the mixed emotions—pride, joy, grief, regret, worry, or nostalgia—that mark this transition. The following blessing for a family may be offered within worship or given to a family to pray at home (by changing the pronouns to "our" or "we").

> Bless your family in the midst of change.
> Bless the home that held your growth.
> Bless the *child/children* that grew within its walls.
> Bless the parents who grew there, too.
>
> Through this time of transition—
> Celebrating joys and lessons learned,
> Forgiving conflicts and losses grieved,
> Giving thanks for memories and blessings shared—
>
> May you learn to let go even as you hold on,
> May you know that love endures even as lives change,
> May you welcome each other whenever you return,
> and may God bless your paths until they meet again.

A Blessing for New Grandparents

Within family life, later adulthood can bring the opportunity to embrace being a grandparent as a new calling. Blessing grandparents at the time of a child's birth, adoption, or baptism is a way for a congregation to celebrate how family members call each other into new vocations.

Your love, O God, is fresh as an infant's, playful as a child's.

Your love, O God, contains the hopefulness of youth and the watchfulness of age.

Your love, O God, is fierce as a mother's, steady as a father's,

loving and wise, O Eldest of elders.

Your love, O God, is present in the love of *N. and N.*,

who, through the *birth/adoption* of [*name of child*],

have become [*great-*] grandparents.

What joys in life compare to this?

Let us share in their joy.

Instruct their hearts in that love you hand down from generation to generation,

from parents through children's children and to every age.

Grant them many years, and descendants as countless as the stars,

and bring us all together, at length,

to the heavenly banquet laid by Jesus,

your Christ and our Savior. Amen.[5]

A Prayer of Calling through Suffering

The process of aging that begins in later adulthood affects body, mind, and spirit. Physical suffering from chronic conditions, serious illness, accidents, or surgery can dramatically alter one's sense of self, relationships, and faith in God. While there are many prayers for pastoral care and healing, prayers about calling in suffering are less common. Yet these experiences of limitation, change, and grief have profound impacts on vocations, both personal and professional. People in pain need to hear that they are called beyond their present suffering into a new reality, that life may be changed but God will remain present. The following blessing may be offered after surgery, sickness, hospitalization, or the death of a loved one.

5. Ibid.

Christ who reached out to those in pain,
>who sat at the bedside of the sick,
>who wept at the death of a beloved friend,
>who agonized in the garden and on the cross,

Christ calls to you now in this present pain.
>He calls you in your fear and suffering.
>He calls you through your anger and grief.
>He calls you as the person you are today.

Christ invites you to dwell within the mystery of God,
>where sorrow becomes joy,
>where fear becomes peace,
>where death becomes life.

May you know Christ as your companion in light and darkness,
now and forever. Amen.

A Prayer for Caregivers

Later adulthood often brings experiences of both giving and receiving care, whether after sickness or surgery or as a new way of life. Caregivers benefit from the support and prayers of their community, especially when the calling is not chosen and its responsibilities stretch their resources and abilities to the limit. Offering a regular blessing of those who give care and those who receive care can frame the experience of caregiving within traditional Christian practices of mercy, comfort, and healing.

God, our refuge and strength,
our present help in time of trouble,
care for those who tend the needs of N.
Strengthen them in body and spirit.
Refresh them when weary;
console them when anxious;
comfort them in grief;
and hearten them in discouragement.
Lord of peace, be with us all,

and give us peace at all times
and in every way. Amen.[6]

A Prayer for Loss in Later Adulthood

Later adulthood brings unbidden changes and unwelcome challenges: the death of relatives and friends, the loss of community after retirement or geographic moves, or the decline of good health. People in later adulthood need to grieve losses as they come to terms with the growing sense of their own mortality. But grief and loss can also be reframed as vocational experiences. There is a call to enter into grief, to journey through suffering, and to integrate loss into life. A congregation that acknowledges this suffering can offer a safe space for adults to grieve and grow. This prayer for loss can be offered in pastoral visits during times of grief or within the funeral rite itself.

> God of grief,
> be our light in darkness,
> our comfort in sorrow,
> our strength in doubt,
> our support in suffering,
> our peace in fear,
> our love in loneliness,
> our hope in despair,
> our healing in pain.
>
> Be for us
> all that this world cannot be:
> lasting joy,
> unfailing love,
> abiding hope,
> enduring peace.

---

6. Presbyterian Church (USA), *Book of Common Worship*, 992.

Help us to trust
in the hope of your name
and the promise of your word.
Amen.

PRAYERS FOR TIMES AND PLACES OF WELCOME

A Blessing for Congregational Leadership

Later adulthood often gives people the time and opportunity to serve in leadership roles in congregations. Thanking members for their wisdom, vision, and dedication is an important way to recognize their church leadership as part of their Christian calling. The following prayer to bless Christian leadership may be used in the commissioning of committee members, the election of church leaders, or the beginning of a new year of church service.

> As you are now called to leadership among us,
> may Christ remain the center of every good purpose,
> for God is redeeming, loving, and renewing.
>
> When the challenges of ministry seem to diminish your focus and
> creativity,
> may the Spirit foster in you an even greater sense of shared pilgrimage,
> for God is revealing who you are and who you are becoming.
>
> When the way forward seems beyond your own strength,
> may the Creator employ your gifts to raise up those around you,
> for God is enlivening our community for service.
>
> When the time comes to wait for clarity and inspiration,
> may you be blessed with the courage to be vulnerable and honest,
> for God is, all the more, cultivating your readiness to lead.[7]

---

7. Rahberg, "Prayer for Christian Leaders."

A Prayer for Social Groups

Social groups, book clubs, and Bible study groups can be important sources of community for those in later adulthood. The calling to friendship is often an overlooked vocation, and church groups provide important opportunities for fellowship, service, and learning in later adulthood. This prayer may be used to open the meetings of social gatherings, whether in the congregation, in members' homes, or elsewhere in your community.

> Lord,
> may everything we do
> begin with your inspiration
> and continue with your help,
> so that all our prayers and words
> may begin in you
> and by you be happily ended.
> We ask this through Christ our Lord.
> Amen.[8]

PETITIONS FOR THE CALLINGS OF LATER ADULTHOOD

Petitions offer a way to encompass the joys and the concerns of later adulthood, which is especially meaningful when people from this stage in life are the ones helping to compose or pray the petitions within worship.

> For the wisdom of mentors, leaders, and all those in our community who offer the gifts of their lived experience.
> For workers who are looking toward retirement; for people who are facing unemployment or underemployment; for those who cannot retire due to financial concerns.

---

8. International Commission on English in the Liturgy, *Book of Blessings*, 190–91.

For the joys of retirement: for time and space to build relationships, explore new interests, and learn from transitions.

For those called to give care and those called to receive it: for a spirit of humility in this exchange of loving service.

For all who are grieving the loss of a spouse, partner, or beloved friend.

For all who are suffering in mind, body, or spirit, especially those whose pain is not easily healed.

For adults in transition, especially those approaching retirement or the newly retired, that they may be open to hear God's call in surprising ways in a new season of life.

For families in the midst of change: for empty nesters, new grandparents, and those who have recently lost a loved one; for families who live close together and families who live far apart.

For grandparents who are raising children: for the strength to do their work anew and for the support of this community to help them.

POEMS TO SPEAK TO LATER ADULTHOOD

The Way It Is

There's a thread you follow. It goes among
things that change. But it doesn't change.
People wonder about what you are pursuing.
You have to explain about the thread.
But it is hard for others to see.
While you hold it you can't get lost.
Tragedies happen; people get hurt
or die; and you suffer and get old.
Nothing you do can stop time's unfolding.
You don't ever let go of the thread.[9]

—WILLIAM STAFFORD

9. Stafford, "Way It Is," 42.

Enduring Ministry: Hope

> God is here and now,
> inviting leaders to maturity.
> Weariness comes from loss of vision—
> the trouble is feeling small.
>
> Shelter your attention to God.
> Leave behind stories of complaint,
> take up stories of pilgrimage,
> remain close to who you are.
>
> Genuine power nurtures
> liveliness and alignment.
> Intentional margins help
> shepherd communities
> toward hope, toward possibility.
>
> Fear distracts us all
> from laying full claim to our lives.
> Look to Christ. Suffer the beautiful
> change that brings new life.[10]

—SAMUEL RAHBERG

HYMNS TO CELEBRATE THE CALLINGS OF LATER ADULTHOOD

God of Our Life, through All the Circling Years

> 1. God of our life, through all the circling years,
> We trust in thee;
> In all the past, through all our hopes and fears,

10. Rahberg, "Enduring Ministry."

Thy hand we see.
With each new day, when morning lifts the veil,
We own thy mercies, Lord, which never fail.

2. God of the past, our times are in thy hand;
With us abide.
Lead us by faith to hope's true promised land;
Be thou our guide.
With thee to bless, the darkness shines as light,
And faith's fair vision changes into sight.

3. God of the coming years, through paths unknown
We follow thee;
When we are strong, Lord, leave us not alone;
Our refuge be.
Be thou for us in life our daily bread,
Our heart's true home when all our years have sped.[11]

SUGGESTED TUNE: SANDON (10.4.10.4.10.10)

How Clear Is Our Vocation, Lord

1. How clear is our vocation, Lord,
when once we heed your call:
to live according to your word,
and daily learn, refreshed, restored,
that you are Lord of all,
and will not let us fall.

2. But if, forgetful, we should find
your yoke is hard to bear;
if worldly pressures fray the mind

11. Kerr, "God of Our Life."

and love itself cannot unwind
its tangled skein of care:
our inward life repair.

3. We mark your saints, how they became
in hindrances more sure,
whose joyful virtues put to shame
the casual way we wear your name,
and by our faults obscure
your power to cleanse and cure.

4. In what you give us, Lord, to do,
together or alone,
in old routines or ventures new,
may we not cease to look for you,
the cross you hung upon,
all you endeavored done.[12]

SUGGESTED TUNE: REPTON (8.6.8.8.6)

12. Green, "How Clear Is Our Vocation, Lord," hymn 580.

6

Prayers for Older Adulthood

OLDER ADULTHOOD IS THE final stage of the lifespan, but it can last for years or decades, making it an important time to continue exploring and living vocation. Older adulthood resists simple stereotypes but is generally identified with declining health and the loss of independence. In contrast to society's vision of the golden years, older adulthood can be a time of struggle and "dis-ease." Major health crises often usher in the shift from later to older adulthood, leading to mobility losses, physical or cognitive impairment, diminishing energy, or chronic pain. Not only is the body experienced as a challenge, but it can also be perceived as an obstacle to participation in society. Emotional health may also change. Older adults often feel overlooked and isolated—at risk for loneliness, depression, and anxiety. Spiritual despair can emerge as older adults wrestle with the existential anguish of "Why am I still here?"

Older adults need the attention and support of caring communities as they journey through their vocational tasks, including life review (coming to terms with joys, sorrows, and regrets of the past), grieving the loss of health and loved ones, celebrating the milestones of long life, and preparing for death. Prayers and books about vocation often overlook older adulthood as a time of calling. But if vocation embraces God's call in our lives all life long, then this dynamic relationship remains through death. Noticing and naming the vocations of older adults is an important way to affirm how callings are not defined by productivity but by faithfulness to the purposes of God.

BLESSINGS FOR MOMENTS AND MILESTONES

A General Blessing for the Calling of Older Adults

The following blessing for older adults gives thanks for their gifts, wisdom, and years of service to those around them. The Scripture references make it an appropriate prayer for the Christmas season (when Jesus was welcomed by Anna and Simeon) or Pentecost (for its emphasis on the Holy Spirit).

> All-knowing and all-loving God,
> whose own dear Son was greeted and blessed by the aged prophets Anna and Simeon:
> Keep us ever mindful of the wisdom and gifts of older adults in our midst;
> enable us to continually grow in love of you
> and service to one another throughout our span of years;
> and, in times of diminishment and loss,
> provide us with compassionate caregivers.
> Fill young and old alike with your Holy Spirit,
> that, as a community of faith,
> we may all share in the accomplishment of your work in the world,
> and together reflect the fullness of your image from generation to generation;
> through Jesus Christ our Lord,
> who lives and reigns with you and the Holy Spirit,
> one God, for ever and ever. Amen.[1]

---

1. Episcopal Diocese of Los Angeles, "Collect and Prayers."

A Prayer for Life Review

As older adults advance in years, they may face fewer discernments of what to do but still wrestle with questions of how to be in this world and where to find God. This is part of the vocational task of life review: working through the past to embrace the future. Life review involves gratitude for the joys of life; grief for losses, regrets, or unfulfilled dreams; forgiveness of self and others; expressions of love to friends and family; and saying goodbye to people and places. While much of this emotional work is done privately, the following prayer in support of this vocational task may be offered as a blessing in worship over older adults present in your congregation or shared during pastoral visits with those who are homebound or hospitalized.

> Lord God almighty,
> bless your servant, *N.*,
> to whom you have given a long life.
> Let *him/her* be aware of your nearness,
> so that, when *he/she* worries about past failings,
> *he/she* will rejoice in your mercy
> and, when *he/she* thinks of the future,
> *he/she* will faithfully rely on you as *his/her* hope.
> We ask this through Christ our Lord.
> Amen.[2]

A Prayer for Transitions in Older Adulthood

Older adulthood brings transitions to almost every aspect of life: family, work, home, activities, physical health, and emotional well-being. A change in one area can trigger unwelcome changes elsewhere, leaving older adults vulnerable to feelings of helplessness or despair. One way to reframe transitions in the light of faith is to ask God's blessing upon the person facing changes, to affirm that they are still valued by their church community. While the following

2. International Commission on English in the Liturgy, *Book of Blessings*, 130.

prayer was written to bless those entering retirement, it can speak to older adults at any time of transition that raises questions of how to spend their time, where to live, or how to deal with the loss of autonomy.

> Gracious God, we thank you for the work and witness of your servant (*name*),
> who has enriched this community and brought gladness to friends and family.
> Now bless and preserve *her/him* at this time of transition.
> Day by day, guide *her/him* and give *her/him* what is needed,
> friends to cheer *her/his* way,
> and a clear vision of that to which you are now calling *her/him*.
> By your Holy Spirit be present in *her/his* pilgrimage,
> that *s/he* may travel with the one who is the way, the truth, and the life,
> Jesus Christ our Lord. Amen.[3]

A Blessing for Moving

Moving from home is a major transition in older adulthood—whether because of the decision to downsize or the need to enter assisted living. Vocations are rooted in places, and our sense of identity and community is anchored by where we live. Saying goodbye to familiar people and places means taking leave of the past and adjusting to new surroundings. Offering a prayer during this emotional transition can remind older adults that the God of comfort also promises to be their companion as they adapt to whatever their future home will hold for them. This blessing can be prayed within worship or to welcome a new resident to a nursing home.

> Sojourning God, you go before *N*. (and *N*.)
> preparing the way to a peaceful new home.
> Give *her* grace to let go of the old,

3. Evangelical Lutheran Church in America, *Evangelical Lutheran Worship*, 82.

accepting the comfort and assistance of those around *her*.
Help *her* know that you are as near as *her* breath;
let *her* hear your whisper of the undying love
in which you hold *her*
as you held *her* in the beginning.
We pray this through Christ our Savior. *Amen.*[4]

A Prayer for Comfort in Suffering

Congregations have a prophetic call to help change the discourse regarding older adulthood. Through preaching and teaching about vocation, you can frame conversations about aging and dying within the context of calling in order to give older adults a safe, sacred space to reflect on mortality. This prayer can speak to people across the lifespan, but its message offers particular comfort for those facing physical or emotional suffering in their later years.

God to surround me, God to encompass me;
God in my words, God in my thought;
God in my waking, God in my resting;
God in my hoping, God in my doing;
God in my heart, God in my soul;
God in my weakness, God in my strength;
God in my life, God in eternity;
God in my life, God in eternity.[5]

A Prayer for Loss in Older Adulthood

Older adulthood brings many goodbyes: to beloved people, to places of work and service, to well-defined roles and responsibilities, and to an independent lifestyle. Some older adults face loss after loss—spouse, friends, relatives—and thoughts of death can

4. Episcopal Church, *Changes*, 54.
5. Calvert, *God to Enfold Me*, 40.

begin to consume their days. Yet there is still a call to move beyond grief into a new experience of life, changed but still offering possibilities for goodness. This prayer about loss serves as a reminder that there is room for lament in the life of faith. Cries of sorrow and anger are part of calling out to God, as heard in the psalms of lament. This prayer may be used during yearly memorial services (or whenever the dead are remembered) as well as regular Sunday worship when Scripture themes speak to death and grief.

> *Response: We bless the Lord, who has shown us love.*
> May God's Spirit touch all amongst us who are widowed,
> who have lost the woman or man we loved and lived for,
> that we can bear our loss in a spirit of gratitude and expectation.
>
> May God's Spirit touch all amongst us
> who are in the autumn of our life,
> that the prospect of aging will not sadden us,
> that we may cling with confidence
> to the One who has always been with us.
>
> May God's Spirit touch all amongst us who are lonely
> from a loss that cannot be compensated for,
> and give us a desire to live
> and a confidence in God's providence.
>
> May God's Spirit touch all amongst us who are disappointed by life,
> for whom life has not always been the joy it can be,
> that we can stay faithful to what we believe
> which is the ultimate mystery of love.
> May God's Spirit be with us as we remember our dead—
> husband or wife, child or parent,
> brother or sister, friend or relation.
> Our communion on earth is our foretaste
> of the communion of saints beyond time and beyond imagination,
> where all the beloved will live love's fullness in God.[6]

6. Harrington, *Prayer Reflections*, 131.

A Prayer to Accompany the Dying

The promises of vocation assure Christians that life holds meaning and purpose up until—and beyond—our earthly end. This blessing to accompany the dying can speak to a variety of situations: praying with the sick who have received a terminal diagnosis, holding vigil with those who are waiting as a loved one dies, or welcoming mourners who gather for a burial. (Chapter 7 on the whole lifespan contains vocation prayers specifically for funerals.)

> God our creator and our end,
> give us grace to bear bravely
> the changes we must undergo,
> the pain we may have to face
> to come to our home with you.
> Give us the courage to welcome
> that unimaginable moment awaiting us;
> give us trust and confidence;
> and at the last give us peace.[7]

PRAYERS FOR TIMES AND PLACES OF WELCOME

Celebrating joyful milestones like wedding anniversaries and birthdays is an important way to support and encourage older adults. An anniversary celebrates not only the married couple but also those they have served over the years by their love. Similarly, a milestone birthday is not simply an achievement of longevity but also an opportunity for all present to give thanks to God as creator and source of life. The following prayers are suited for worship, grace before a celebratory meal, or other gatherings of fellowship.

---

7. Anglican Church in Aotearoa, New Zealand and Polynesia, *New Zealand Prayer Book*, 748.

A Blessing for a Wedding Anniversary

> You unite your people in marriage, O God,
> delighting in us as the joyful bride of your heart.
> In the union of *N.* and *N.*, we remember your faithfulness,
> and the tender love in which you hold and behold us for ever.
> Calling them together,
> you have helped them make their love a strong rock
> on which they have built a sacred companionship.
> You have granted them moments and days and now _____ years of blessedness.
> We rejoice in their contentment, promising to support and honor them.
> We ask that our own loves may display the constancy of theirs.
> Protect them this day and always,
> as together they grow in your likeness and grace;
> through Christ who blessed the wedding feast at Cana. *Amen.*[8]

A Blessing for a Milestone Birthday

> God of passionate youth and seasoned age,
> You are our dwelling place in all generations.
> In this moment we stop to thank you for *name(s)*
> who have lived to see their *ninetieth* birthday.
> You are our dwelling place in all generations.
> We rejoice in *their* youth when you blessed *them*
> with identity, vision, and lasting relationships.
> You are our dwelling place in all generations.
> We rejoice in their productive years of work and service,
> *and marriage and family.*
> You are our dwelling place in all generations.
> We rejoice in your calling *them* to be your disciples and

8. Episcopal Church, *Changes*, 53.

for *their* lives of love and holy habits.
You are our dwelling place in all generations.
We thank you for the struggles *they* endured
and the temptations *they* resisted.
You are our dwelling place in all generations.
We thank you for your mercy toward *them* and us
in our failures and foolishness.
You are our dwelling place in all generations.
This day we thank you that they are among us as
witnesses of endurance and wisdom that comes with seeing a lot
    of life.
You are our dwelling place in all generations.
May *they* live at peace with *themselves* and with you
trusting your love and care all *their* days.
You are our dwelling place in all generations.[9]

A Prayer for Senior Groups

Senior groups are popular sources of fellowship within congregations. These groups provide an important part of the callings of older adulthood: to friendship, to continuing forms of service, and to the emotional support of their peers in the wider community. Although senior groups meet in a variety of contexts, opening or closing in prayer is a common practice. This blessing speaks to the shared Christian calling of all those gathered.

Lord, as we prepare to begin our meeting,
we recall your promise to be present
when two or three are gathered in your name.
We know that without you here among us,
and within each one of us,
we will labour in vain.
All: Unite us, Lord, in your Spirit.

9. Discipleship Ministries of the United Methodist Church, "Litany."

We rejoice that we are blessed and called together
to work in your name.
We pray that we will respond generously
to this opportunity to serve you
and that we will grow in our Christian calling.
All: Unite us, Lord, in your Spirit.

Inspire us with your Spirit of wisdom;
plant seeds of your vision in our hearts and minds;
give us humour and give us humility
in our working with one another,
so that we may know the privilege of participating
in the coming about of your Kingdom.
All: Unite us, Lord, in your Spirit.

We ask that working together
will increase the communion among us
as members of your Body on earth.
May the communion we experience
give us new courage in all that we do for you.
All: Unite us, Lord, in your Spirit.

Grant us the willingness to be open to each other,
to respect each other,
to listen to each other,
to be honest with each other
to be supportive of each other,
for the sake of your Kingdom.
All: Unite us, Lord, in your Spirit.[10]

10. Harrington and Kavanagh, *Prayer for Parish Groups*, 172–73.

PETITIONS FOR THE CALLINGS OF OLDER ADULTHOOD

Praying for the needs and concerns of older adults offers a way to turn from fear and toward trust in the faithful promises and presence of God—which are at the heart of vocation.

> For the service of older adults to the church and wider community, and for our continued welcome of their gifts and desire to serve.
>
> For the joys of older adulthood: for the gift of volunteer service or leisure activities, for the opportunity to travel; for the chance to spend time with grandchildren or relatives; for the blessing of friends and the support of peers.
>
> For the gifts of grandparents, great-grandparents, and all older adults who love and mentor the young.
>
> For courage and strength for those facing difficult decisions in old adulthood, and for the loving support of their family and friends through these transitions.
>
> For those with chronic conditions or terminal illness, and those who care for them; for patience, strength, and deep love, even on the most difficult days.
>
> For older adults suffering from loneliness, depression, isolation, or anxiety, and for those facing fears about health concerns or financial need.
>
> For men and women with dementia or cognitive loss, that they might know their dignity and worth as created by God, that they may be loved beyond their ability to do or communicate.
>
> For those who are dying; for their family and friends preparing to mourn; and for all who will die alone today.
>
> For those afraid of death or uncertain about the afterlife, that God's calming peace may be their companion through their questions and fears.

POEMS THAT SPEAK TO OLDER ADULTHOOD

We Look with Uncertainty

> We look with uncertainty
> beyond the old choices for
> clear-cut answers
> to softer, more permeable aliveness
> which is every moment
> at the brink of death;
> for something new is being born in us
> if we but let it.
> We stand in a new doorway,
> awaiting that which comes . . .
> daring to be human creatures,
> vulnerable to the beauty of existence.
> Learning to love.[11]

—ANNE HILLMAN

HYMNS TO CELEBRATE THE CALLINGS OF OLDER ADULTHOOD

God, We Spend a Lifetime Growing

> God, we spend a lifetime growing, learning of your love and care,
> Planting seeds you give for sowing, working for the fruit they'll bear.
> Now we honor faithful servants who, with joy, look back and see
> Years of growing in your presence, lives of fruitful ministry.

11. Hillman, "We Look with Uncertainty," 215.

Thank you, Lord, for ones who teach us what has brought them to this place!

May their faith-filled witness reach us; may we glimpse in them your grace.

Strong in you, their strength uplifts us from our birth until life's end;

Spirit-filled, they give us gifts, as prophet, mentor, guide, and friend.

Christ our Lord, you walk beside us, giving daily work to do;

Years go by and still you guide us as we seek to follow you.

If our sight fails, weak hands tremble, minds forget the things we've known,

Lord, we trust that you remember, hold us close, and see us home.[12]

SUGGESTED TUNE: HYMN TO JOY (8.7.8.7.)

For Each Day of Life We Thank Thee

1. For each day of life we thank you,
God, the giver of all days;
and with hearts filled with thanksgiving,
we would serve you, now, always.

2. As in days of youthful vigor,
may we in all later years
know the joys of useful purpose.
Free us from our anxious fears.

3. Give us dreams and inner vision
of a new world to be gained,
where all people live together,
by each other's love sustained.

4. May the insights from living
be a light upon the way,

12. Gillette, "God, We Spend a Lifetime Growing."

93

guiding us, and those to follow,
to a brighter, better day.[13]

SUGGESTED TUNE: GALILEE (8.7.8.7.)

13. Lanier, "For Each Day of Life We Thank Thee."

7

Prayers across the Lifespan

FROM THE YOUNGEST BABIES to the oldest adults, all ages and stages of life gather in church together. Unlike many places in society where people are segregated by age (such as schools or retirement communities), congregations still remain common ground for people to meet across their different experiences. In addition to praying for the particular callings of each stage of life, your community can also join together to celebrate the shared Christian vocation of all gathered in worship. The following prayers and hymns can be used to speak to the common concerns of Christians across the lifespan, from childhood through older adulthood.

PRAYERS FOR WORSHIP

A Call to Worship

O God,
you who gave us birth
and who will walk with us through our older years,
we come to you today to worship and praise you.
We call your name and you answer us.
In every age of life
you give us what we need.

Help us today to have ears to hear the message of your faithfulness,
and to celebrate the ways in which you help us
to cope with the challenges we face at every age.
Surround this congregation today
with your presence, your love, your grace.
We pray this in Jesus's name. Amen.[1]

A Call to Worship and Invocation

Call to Worship
One: From ages young and old, and in-between,
All: we come to worship the Lord.
One: It is you, O Lord, who gives us life and guides our paths,
as we move from one age to another,
All: and in your right hand we find rest and joy.
One: Make us aware of your presence this day,
All: and open our lives to your glory.
One: Lift us from trouble and despair,
All: for your path leads to joy and life.

Invocation
O God, you who are the author of all life,
and who knows the path of life that lies out before us,
we desire to be in your presence.
We may come as little children or as older adults, or any age,
but we have come desiring to be filled
with the joy that comes from being held
in your hands of creation.
Create in us hearts that can rejoice
regardless of where we find ourselves on this path of life.
May we receive the blessings of life
that flow through the relationships we have

1. Caring Ministries of the Church of the Brethren, "Calls to Worship."

with Jesus and with one another.
In Jesus's name we pray. Amen.[2]

A Prayer of Thanksgiving

God of every goodness,
We give you thanks for all that gives life its savor:
    for work done well, and rest;
    for good food, and strength we draw from it;
    for familiar things, and new;
    for the spring of youth, and age's season;
    for the touch of loved ones, and the kindness of strangers;
    for times of gathering with your people in prayer,
    and the prayer we carry into work, school, and home;
    for the spoken word, and silence.
God of every, every goodness,
hear our thanks. Amen.[3]

A Litany of Thanksgiving

Give thanks to the Lord who is good.
God's love is everlasting.

Come, let us praise God joyfully.
Let us come to God with thanksgiving.

For the good world;
for things great and small, beautiful and awesome;
for seen and unseen splendors;
Thank you, God.

---

2. Caring Ministries of the Church of the Brethren, "Journey."
3. Williams, *Worship and Daily Life*, 31.

Part 1: Ages and Stages

For human life;
for talking and moving and thinking together;
for common hopes and hardships shared from birth until our dying;
Thank you, God.

For work to do and strength to work;
for the comradeship of labor;
for exchanges of good humor and encouragement;
Thank you, God.

For marriage;
for the mystery and joy of flesh made one;
for mutual forgiveness and burdens shared;
for secrets kept in love;
Thank you, God.

For family;
for living together and eating together;
for family amusements and family pleasures;
Thank you, God.

For children;
for their energy and curiosity;
for their brave play and startling frankness;
for their sudden sympathies;
Thank you, God.

For the young;
for their high hopes;
for their irreverence toward worn-out values;
for their search for freedom;
for their solemn vows;
Thank you, God.

For growing up and growing old;
or wisdom deepened by experience;
for rest in leisure;
and for time made precious by its passing;
Thank you, God.

For your help in times of doubt and sorrow;
for healing our diseases;
for preserving us in temptation and danger;
Thank you, God.

For the church into which we have been called;
for the good news we receive by Word and Sacrament;
for our life together in the Lord;
We praise you, God.

For your Holy Spirit,
who guides our steps and brings us gifts of faith and love;
who prays in us and prompts our grateful worship;
We praise you, God.

Above all, O God, for your Son Jesus Christ,
who lived and died and lives again for our salvation;
for our hope in him;
and for the joy of serving him;
We thank and praise you, Eternal God,
for all your goodness to us.

Give thanks to the Lord, who is good.
God's love is everlasting.[4]

---

4. Presbyterian Church (USA), *Book of Common Worship*, 792–93.

A Communal Prayer for Discernment

Reflection
Each of us makes our life decisions;
each of us chooses a path to follow,
a value to live by,
another to love.
Each of us chooses and is chosen,
each of us both takes a path and is shown a path.
For some of us, the choice lies ahead,
for others it is long since made;
others again are wrestling with deciding,
others are reviewing and choosing again.
In quiet prayer, we place our commitments before you, Lord,
you who have committed yourself completely to us.

Prayer
We pray to the God of promise and expectation
to bless our commitments, whatever point they are at,
whether we are assured or struggling,
surviving or rejoicing
or still exploring.

God our creator,
in Jesus Christ you have bound yourself to humanity
in a bond that cannot be broken.
From earliest times, your people called you
"rock" and "stronghold" and "mighty fortress,"
as they came to appreciate
your absolute loyalty and utter dependability.
In Jesus's heart of love you have given the world
the enduring statement, that you are everlasting, faithful love.

In all the power of who you are,
bless each one here on the journey of commitment.
Bless each one with the gifts
that will enhance their joy on the journey—
the gift of listening,
the gift of putting others first,
the gift of self-knowledge,
the gift of reliability and faithfulness,
the gift of energy,
the gift of reflection.

As you bless us, may each of us experience,
in our hearts and in our lives, even a shadow or a hint
of the unspeakable, incomparable mystery of love that you are.

As you bless us, we bless you
for all that you mean to us, through Jesus Christ our Lord.[5]

PRAYERS FOR SPECIAL OCCASIONS

Prayers for Weddings

For *N.* and *N.* in their new calling as a married couple, that they will listen together for God's call in their lives and respond with love to those who need their gifts and service.

For all who helped raise and teach *N.* and *N.*; for the parents, grandparents, friends, relatives, and mentors who have supported them; and for all those they will serve by their life together.

For all whose work, energy, and talents have made *N.* and *N.*'s wedding day a beautiful and joyful celebration.

For the families of *N.* and *N.*, who today welcome a new member, that they will be blessed with open hearts and generous spirits through this time of change and growth.

---

5. Harrington, *Prayer Reflections*, 124–25.

Prayers for Funerals

The word *eulogy*—from the Greek *eulogia*—means to praise or to speak well of. During a funeral, speaking well of the dead by praising the work and relationships to which they gave their time and energy is a powerful witness. The following examples of prayers for various vocations are meant to inspire a congregation's petitions for their deceased. While not every occupation or situation can be represented here, the wide range of work and service celebrated in these funeral prayers can be adapted to speak to the particular life, work, and relationships of the one who has died.

All prayers may be followed by this or other suitable responses:

We pray to the Lord . . . Lord, hear our prayer.

Or, Lord, in your mercy . . . Hear our prayer.

> *For administrative/support staff: Name* worked as *a/n [specify occupation]*, contributing *his/her* talents to serve and support others. May *he/she* now enter into the joy of *his/her* Master.

> *For an administrator, manager, or coordinator:* As *a/n [specify], name* exercised *his/her* talents in administration; may *he/she* now hear Christ say, "You were faithful in small matters. . . . Come, share your Master's joy."

> *For an artist:* Through *name*'s art, we saw the creative spark come alive; may *he/she* now rejoice in being near to God, the Source of the creative fire.

> *For a builder/construction worker:* Through *his/her* profession as a builder, *name* provided housing for many people. Now may *he/she* come into God's house and dwell there forever.

> *For a business owner or employee:* As *name* served the community in the *[specify]* business, may *his/her* service now be honored in the community of the saints.

> *For a caregiver:* During *his/her* life, *name* lovingly and faithfully cared for others *[or specify a person]*; now may *he/she* know the wonderful bounty of God's loving care for *him/her*.

For a cook or food service worker: Name prepared food to provide nourishment and hospitality to others; may *he/she* now relish the heavenly banquet in God's kingdom.

For a doctor: In life, people came to *name* seeking healing; now as *he/she* comes into the presence of God, may *he/she* experience the love from which all healing comes.

For an emergency worker: Daily, *name* risked laying down *his/her* life for others; grant *him/her* now the fullness of joy that comes from Christ's laying down his life for us.

For a farmer: Name lived close to the earth. *He/she* watched the coming of the seasons and the passing of the years with their sowing and sprouting, ripening and harvesting. May *he/she* now present to God the good harvest of *his/her* life.

For a firefighter: As in the story of Daniel's friends in the fiery furnace, *name* was challenged to walk into the heart of the flames and be protected by God. May God's protection surround *name's* family at this time of grief.

For a health care provider or mental health provider: On earth, in *his/her* service as *a/n [specify occupation], name* saw you and loved you in the faces of the troubled, sick, and grieving. Now may *he/she* have the joy of seeing you and loving you face to face in heaven.

For a homemaker: Name devoted *himself/herself* to making a home for those *he/she* loved. Grant *him/her* now a place of honor in your heavenly dwelling.

For a judge: In this life, *name* sat in judgment receiving the testimony of those who came as witnesses before *him/her*. May *he/ she* now stand honorably before God, the Judge of the living and the dead, as witness to *his/her* own life in Christ.

For a lawyer: As *name* brought cases before earthly judges, may *he/she* now bring evidence before the Divine Judge that during life *he/she* acted justly, loved tenderly, and walked humbly with our God.

For a musician: Making music before the Lord was a part of *name's* life on earth. May *he/she* now join the harmonious voice of eternal glory.

For a nurse: Name extended help and comfort to those suffering from illness; may *he/she* now know the powerful compassion of the Divine Physician.

For a police officer: As *name* sought to protect others, may *he/she* now know the protection of God's holy presence.

For a public servant or government employee: In life, *name* participated in governing and exercising authority in the name of the common good; may *he/she* now enjoy the greatest good, the kingdom of heaven.

For a salesperson: Name found challenge and vitality in *his/her* work in sales; may *he/she* now find new delight in God's embrace.

For a scholar or scientist: In *his/her* work as *a/n [specify], name* grew to know and be in awe of God's universe. May *he/she* now experience the wonder of knowing the wisdom of God's design.

For a social worker or advocate for the oppressed: During this life, *name* shared the burdens of the oppressed and worked that they might be freed from their distress. Grant that *his/her* work might bear much fruit and give *him/her* the eternal joy won for us by Jesus, our Liberator.

For a teacher or professor: May *name*, who devoted *his/her* life to teaching others, now sit with joy at the feet of Jesus, our Teacher.

For a volunteer: As a volunteer, *name* emulated Jesus in *his/her* life of service. May our Lord, the humble Servant, now welcome *name* into his kingdom.

For a writer: Name sought to express meaning through words; may *he/she* now enjoy the inexpressible fullness of God's love, the source of all meaning.[6]

---

6. Michalek and Fader, *Blessed Are Those Who Mourn*, 20–42.

HYMNS ON VOCATION ACROSS THE LIFESPAN

Call Us, One and All, Together

1. Gracious God, your love has found us,
bound us, set us free.
Take our lives, transform us into
all that we can be.
Refrain:
Call us, one and all, together,
now and evermore, we pray.

2. Call us to be Christ-revealing,
radiant with your light;
generous as a hilltop city,
visible and bright.

3. Call us all to live the kingdom,
active here and now;
Life affirming, world-renewing.
Church above, below.

4. Call us all in love discerning,
strong in word and deed;
sent, commissioned, gladly serving
all who are in need.

5. Call us as your loved disciples:
learning, growing, fed;
Send us out, as new apostles,
Leading as we're led.

6. Call us deeply, touch our souls through
worship, prayer and word,
teach our minds to feel in echo
myst'ries yet unheard.

7. Call us, as you called creation
when the world began,
Guide our hearts' imagination
to your loving plan.[7]

SUGGESTED TUNE: GUITING POWER
(8.5.8.5 WITH REFRAIN)

God of Ages

God of ages, times and seasons,
    light that shines through all that lives,
yours the spirit which empowers,
    yours the caring heart that gives
confidence to face the future,
    strengthens faith when courage wanes,
challenges to new endeavors,
    when we doubt, our hope sustains.

God of galaxies and planets
    far beyond all human thought,
centuries, like pages turning,
    are within your keeping brought.
You, the past that makes our present,
    you the future still concealed,
yours the sacrificial giving,
    boundless love through Christ revealed.

God, Creator, Holy Spirit,
    Word made flesh in Christ, your Son
whose example we would follow
    so that all might be as one—

---

7. Barrett, "Hymns."

ever loving, ever hopeful
of a world redeemed, restored;
people, by their faith united,
dedicated to their Lord.

God, the Alpha and Omega,
source of wisdom, life and breath,
you our highest motivation,
you the love that conquers death.
In past ages people sought you;
you are with us now as then.
In your hands we leave the future,
God, our ultimate AMEN.[8]

SUGGESTED TUNE: AUSTRIAN HYMN (8.7.8.7 D)

Hope of Our Calling: Hope through Courage Won

Hope of our calling: hope through courage won;
By those who dared to share all Christ had done.
Saints of today, Christ's banner now unfurled,
We bring his gospel to a waiting world.

Hope of our calling: hope with strength empowered,
Inspired by all that we have seen and heard;
This call is ours, for we are chosen too,
To live for God in all we say and do.

Hope of our calling: hope with grace outpoured,
From death's despair the gift of life restored;
Our call to serve, to wash each other's feet,
To bring Christ's healing touch to all we meet.

8. Marshall, "God of Ages."

Hope of our calling: hope by faith made bold;
To sow God's righteousness throughout the world;
Bring peace from conflict, fruitfulness from weeds,
The kingdom's harvest from the kingdom's seeds.

Hope of our calling: Spirit-filled, unbound,
Old joys remembered and new purpose found,
Our call refreshed by sacrament and word,
We go in peace to love and serve the Lord.[9]

SUGGESTED TUNE: WOODLANDS (10.10.10.10)

Lord of Our Growing Years

1. Lord of our growing years,
With us from infancy,
Laughter and quick-dried tears,
Freshness and energy:

Refrain:
Your grace surrounds us all our days;
For all Your gifts we bring our praise.

2. Lord of our strongest years,
Stretching our youthful powers,
Lovers and pioneers
When all the world seems ours:

3. Lord of our middle years,
Giver of steadfastness,
Courage that perseveres
When there is small success:

9. Barrett, "Hymns."

4. Lord of our older years,
Steep though the road may be,
Rid us of foolish fears,
Bring us serenity:

5. Lord of our closing years,
Always Your promise stands;
Hold us, when death appears,
Safely within Your hands.[10]

SUGGESTED TUNE: LITTLE CORNARD
(6.6.6.6.8.8)

We Enter Your Church, Lord

We enter your church, Lord, through welcoming doors.
We enter it, too, where you claim us as yours.
It's here at the font that you offer a sign:
You tell us, "My children, you're baptized! You're mine!"

O God, you have called us, inviting us in;
You've made us your household and freed us from sin.
From youngest to oldest, we find in this place
Your waters of welcome, your family, your grace.

We've heard here your welcome and also your call;
Your Spirit inspires us to share Christ with all.
The life we receive here is life we can share;
We'll carry your message of love everywhere.[11]

SUGGESTED TUNE: CRADLE SONG
(11.11.11.11)

10. Mowbray, "Lord of Our Growing Years," hymn 556.
11. Gillette, "We Enter Your Church, Lord."

A Hymn of Calling

For all that we are called to,
God, we give thanks this day.
For people, partners, places,
at home, at work, at play.
You bless us for our callings
and make the world's needs known.
Give us the strength and courage
to serve where we are shown.

The people we are called as,
diverse and none the same.
Created for vocation,
baptized and called by name.
To witness as disciples,
our universal call,
Yet each uniquely serving
the God who cares for all.

The struggles we are called in,
the grief that wounds us all,
In sickness, loss, and hardship,
help us discern your call.
As challenge shapes vocation,
our lives are carved by change.
Walk with us when we suffer,
transform us through our pain.

To You, God, we sing praises,
the One who calls each one.
Transforming and inviting,
you call and we respond.
Creator and Redeemer,
the Spirit's stirring song—

Your Trinity uniting
to call our whole life long.[12]

Suggested tune: AURELIA
(7.6.7.6 D)

12. Fanucci, "Hymn of Calling."

PART 2

Work and Profession

For we are God's servants, working together;
you are God's field, God's building.

—1 COR 3:9

CONGREGATIONS ARE CALLED TO preach, bless, name, and notice
people's work. Communities of faith cannot afford to spend a minor-
ity of time concerned with what the majority of its members spend
the majority of their time doing—work. The contexts, conditions,
and consequences of work touch nearly every aspect of Christian life
and identity, including expression of one's gifts, love of neighbor, ethical conduct, issues of justice, and commitment to the common good.

Part 2 offers prayers and blessings to celebrate and support
vocations to work. Chapter 8 introduces a collection of general
blessings, litanies, and petitions for work suitable for use in worship and other congregational gatherings. Chapter 9 presents
prayers for particular professions and a calendar for blessing various professional groups throughout the year. Chapter 10 lays out
a ritual for blessing professionals that can be adapted to any group
of workers. Underlying all these resources is an abiding incarna-
tional belief that God's work in the world, in which every Christian
is called to participate, can be done in businesses, homes, offices,
restaurants, fields, factories, schools, and stores.

8

Prayers for Work

CONGREGATIONS HAVE AN INFLUENTIAL role in helping people connect work and faith. While historically some Christian traditions collapsed vocation into work, today it is more common to hear parishioners say that they rarely hear about their work life from the pulpit. People long to understand how to bring faith into their work in authentic ways, especially within complicated and even corrupt situations in which employees find themselves. Many are hungry for guidance in navigating complex institutions, ethical dilemmas, and everyday conflicts in their workplaces. Vocation provides a framework to raise important questions about work-life balance, justice and ethical living, gifts and responsibilities, and service of the common good.

This chapter offers a variety of prayers that speak to work as a vital concern for the Christian community. These blessings, litanies, and petitions hold up those who work and those who are served by their work, as well as those beginning new jobs, changing careers, working in unpaid roles, transitioning into retirement, and facing unemployment or underemployment. Ultimately, the call to your congregation is to discern how to help each member respond to God's call within and through their work for the well-being of the wider community.

PRAYERS FOR OPENING WORSHIP

Acknowledging work as a place from which people come to worship and return afterward builds a bridge and breaks down false dichotomies between what is holy and what is not. Each of the three prayers below could be used as a call to worship or an opening prayer for church meetings or adult education sessions. The first two connect human work with God's creative work, asking God's blessing upon daily labor. The third prayer celebrates the diversity of workplaces from which people gather to worship. (You could also substitute references to workplaces that are familiar to your congregation's members and community.)

> Eternal God, who has created all things
> > good and beautiful and true,
> > teach us so to honor your creative work
> > in all we think and say and do,
> > that our worship may become seamless with our lives,
> > and our lives with your good purposes.
> Through Jesus Christ we pray. Amen.[1]

> Eternal God,
> our beginning and our end,
> be our starting point and our haven,
> and accompany us in this day's journey.
> Use our hands
> to do the work of your creation,
> and use our lives
> to bring others the new life you give this world
> in Jesus Christ, Redeemer of all.[2]

> From the highway and from the skies,
> from the office and from the streets,
> from the jail and from the classroom,

1. Williams, *Worship and Daily Life*, 50.
2. Presbyterian Church (USA), *Book of Common Worship*, 500.

from the kitchen and from the garage,
from the bank and from the gym,
from the table and from the font
a voice beckons.
May we hear and may we follow.[3]

LITANIES FOR WORK

Petitions offer a direct, simple way to pray for people's work. The brief format allows for lifting up a profession's gifts to the human community or the struggles of individuals within their work. Your congregation could adopt the practice of including one particular profession or type of work within its prayers of the people each Sunday. Litanies also offer a prayerful, poetic way to bless the gifts of work and intercede for injustices. The following litanies can be used within worship (for example, to acknowledge Labor Day) or as an opening or closing prayer for a church committee meeting.

Leader: We pray this day for all who labor,
People: which includes all of us.
Leader: For those who work with their hands.
People: For those who work with their minds.
Leader: For those who work with their families.
People: For those who look for work.
Leader: For those who seek to find their next meal.
People: For those who help others find their next meal.
Leader: For those who care for their homes.
People: For those who give away their time freely.
Leader: For those who work to live.
People: For those who live to work.
Leader: All of us are given work.
People: Let us thank the Lord no matter what the work.
All: Amen.[4]

3. Williams, *Worship and Daily Life*, 18.
4. Ibid., 61.

Part 2: Work and Profession

Leader: O Lord God: you are ever at work in the world for us and
   for all humankind.

Guide and protect all who work to get their living.

People: Amen.

Leader: For those who plow the earth,

For those who tend machinery;

People: Work with them, O God.

Leader: For those who sail deep waters,

For those who venture into space;

People: Work with them, O God.

Leader: For those who work in offices and warehouses,

For those who labor in stores or factories;

People: Work with them, O God.

Leader: For those who work in mines,

For those who buy and sell;

People: Work with them, O God.

Leader: For those who entertain us,

For those who broadcast or publish;

People: Work with them, O God.

Leader: For those who keep house,

For those who train children;

People: Work with them, O God.

Leader: For all who live by strength of arm,

For all who live by skill of hand;

People: Work with them, O God.

Leader: For all who employ or govern;

People: Work with them, O God.

Leader: For all who excite our minds with art, science, or learning;
People: Work with them, O God.

Leader: For all who instruct,
For writers and teachers;
People: Work with them, O God.

Leader: For all who serve the public good in any way by working;
People: Work with them, O God.

Leader: For all who labor without hope,
For all who labor without interest;
For those who have too little leisure,
For those who have too much leisure;
For those who are underpaid,
For those who pay small wages;
For those who cannot work,
For those who look in vain for work;
For those who trade on the troubles of others,
For profiteers, extortioners, and greedy people;
People: Great God: we pray your mercy, grace, and saving power.

Leader: Work through us and help us always to work for you; in Jesus Christ our Lord.
People: Amen.[5]

PRAYERS FOR WORK AS VOCATION

The following prayers include general themes centered on work, making them appropriate for many forms of worship, including most Sundays. The mention of the common good in each prayer also reminds worshipers that the ultimate aim of work is to serve the purposes of God at work in the world.

---

5. Rowthorn, *Wideness of God's Mercy*, 249–50.

Almighty God our heavenly Father, you declare your glory and
show forth your handiwork in the heavens and in the earth: Deliver us in our various occupations from the service of self alone,
that we may do the work you give us to do in truth and beauty
and for the common good; for the sake of him who came among
us as one who serves, your Son Jesus Christ our Lord, who lives
and reigns with you and the Holy Spirit, one God, for ever and
ever. *Amen.*[6]

Loving God, you made us co-creators in the process of your creation,
blessing us with wisdom, reason, creativity, and skill.
Bless all who seek meaningful employment
that they might provide for the well-being of their families.
Let those who have more than they need for life's necessities
be moved to use their wealth to create new opportunities for others.
Let those who have skills
be open to sharing the riches of their knowledge
with those who seek the opportunity to learn.
Let us all learn from one another,
for you have blessed every human being
with a gift for the benefit of the common good.
And thereby enable us
by the power of your Holy Spirit
to build up the body of Christ on this earth
that your name may be proclaimed and blessed
through the good work of all;
in Christ's name we pray. Amen.[7]

PRAYERS FOR DIFFICULTY IN WORK

Prayers for work cannot simply bless a glowing ideal. Every vocation bring challenges and demands, sacrifice and compromise. For
some people, work can mean unsafe or unjust working conditions;

6. Episcopal Church, *Book of Common Prayer*, 261.

7. Anderson, *Prayers of Our Hearts*, 45.

others struggle to find suitable employment. The following prayers bring these needs and laments within worship by addressing unemployment, underemployment, and the complexities of work in people's lives.

> Heavenly Father,
> we remember before you
> those who suffer want and anxiety from lack of work.
> Guide the people of this land
> so to use our public and private wealth
> that all people may find suitable and fulfilling employment
> and receive just payment for their labor;
> through your Son, Jesus Christ our Lord. Amen.[8]

O God, the heavens declare your glory and tell of your work in creation. From you come the gifts of our bodies and minds, our skills and abilities, and the opportunities to use these gifts in sustaining our lives and in helping our neighbors. We pray for those whose livelihood is insecure; for those who are bearing heavy burdens and stressful times at work; for those whose work is tedious or dangerous; for those who have experienced failures at work; for those who have lost a job; and for all who face any difficulty in their lives of labor. Surround them with your never-failing love; free them from restlessness and anxiety; keep them in every perplexity and distress; and renew them in facing the opportunities and challenges of daily life and work; through Jesus Christ, our Savior and Lord.[9]

PRAYERS FOR THOSE WHOSE WORK IS NOT PAID

Supporting people whose work is not paid or recognized in formal ways, such as caregivers and at-home parents, is important for congregations. The following prayers offer both general and specific blessings for this vocational work. By including unpaid work

---

8. Episcopal Church, *Book of Common Prayer*, 824.
9. Evangelical Lutheran Church in America, *Pastoral Care*, 376.

as part of people's callings, the definition of vocation is stretched to embrace more ways that God is at work in the world.

God of boundless love,
your care for us comes through the hands of others.
Today we pray for all who do the hands-on work of love:
those whose daily labor is in the home,
those who care for young and old,
those who tend bodies, minds, and hearts in need.
We pray in a special way
for all who give care but do not receive pay,
those whose work continues round the clock.
those whose labor can be dirty and demanding.
May they know their work is worthy.
May they feel your presence
as they take up their daily tasks.
May they be supported by this community
and our common call:
to love our neighbor,
to care for the least among us,
and to do unto others as Christ did for us.
In the name of your Son,
who washed feet to show love,
we pray. Amen.

God of compassion, this day we especially give thanks for those who serve others without receiving payment for their work: those who volunteer to help the homeless, sick, lonely, hungry, disabled, imprisoned, and deprived people of our world; those who work with children and adults to give them new opportunities for learning and development; those who help us be better citizens and keep the important issues before our communities; those who work to save our environment and precious resources; those who spend their time supporting your work in the world with prayer.

Help these givers of gifts rely on you for energy, renewal, and strength. May they be able to walk with those they serve as humble servants in Christ's name. We thank you for their call to this work,

and we ask that they may know your presence and be aware of the
prayers given for them by this community of faith. *Amen.*[10]

Blessed are you, Lord, God of mercy,
who through your Son gave us a marvelous example of charity
and the great commandment of love for one another.
Send down your blessings on these your servants,
who so generously devote themselves to helping others.
When they are called on in times of need,
let them faithfully serve you in their neighbor.

We ask this through Christ our Lord.
Amen.[11]

PRAYERS FOR SENDING FORTH

The moment of sending forth from worship is a fitting time to
name the connections between what is preached and what is prac-
ticed, so that people can see the whole of their lives—and not only
their participation in church—as a faithful response to God's call.
The following prayers can be used at the end of Sunday worship or
other church gatherings.

God of goodness,
Your Son called his disciples to follow
in the midst of their daily work.
So, too, you call each of us today to give our lives:
to love, to work, and to serve your people.
As we go forth from this place,
let our callings be joined in response to your call:
our "yes"—at home, at work, and at play—
to the fullness of life that you offer.

10. Williams, *Worship and Daily Life*, 59.
11. International Commission on English in the Liturgy, *Book of Blessings*, 208.

May we give the whole of ourselves and our lives
to the redeeming work of your Spirit in our world,
and may our homes and workplaces
be changed by the vision of your hope and love.
We ask this through Christ our Lord. Amen.

Leader: Lord, your love has brought us here,
People: By your love send us forth.
Leader: May your love be active in us
as we wake or sleep, work or rest, serve or wait.
*People: Draw us by the needs of others into the way, the truth, and
the life we see in Christ.*
All: We follow in faith. Amen.[12]

PRAYERS FOR PERSONAL OR GROUP USE

The following prayers are suitable for use outside worship (for example, to open a Bible study or pray line by line around the table at a meeting) and can be offered by parishioners as morning blessings to call upon God as the work day begins and offer the good of the day to God. As vocational prayers they move beyond personal spirituality to connect work to the common good.

God: be with us all day,
in streets or buildings where we work,
so that everything we do may be for you,
and your Son, our Lord, Jesus Christ. Amen.[13]

Gracious God, as we start this workday we are reminded of the fullness of the day that stretches before us. We are aware of the gift of time and the many things that we will do with this time today. We are aware of the many people our work affects and the web of relationships that encompasses our daily work. We are

12. Williams, *Worship and Daily Life*, 75.
13. Joint Committee on Worship, *Worshipbook*, 205.

aware of the needs that our work revolves around. We pray to be attentive to such needs and concerns. *Amen.*[14]

HYMNS ABOUT WORK AND PROFESSIONS

O God, Our Creator, You Work Every Day

O God, our Creator, you work every day:
A potter, you form us, your people, like clay.
A shepherd, you guide us and seek out the lost.
A parent, you love us, not counting the cost.

Christ Jesus, how rough were your hard-working hands!
You labored among us; our God understands!
Bless workers who struggle, their families to feed;
Bless those who face hardship, oppression, or greed.

Lord, some live among us who need constant care,
Whose work is to make us more humbly aware.
They teach us the best of your lessons, by far:
It's not what we do, Lord, you love who we are!

We're baptized! Your Spirit gives new work to do,
That we, through our serving, may glorify you.
Each person's vocation, each calling, has worth
As you send us out to bring Christ's love on earth.[15]

SUGGESTED TUNE: ST. DENIO (11.11.11.11)

14. Williams, *Worship and Daily Life*, 51.
15. Gillette, "O God, Our Creator, You Work Every Day."

Part 2: Work and Profession

God of Work

God of work, who works within us,
Each new day our strength renew.
When life's burdens seem too heavy
May we put our trust in you.
Guide our mind, inspire our thinking;
Guide our hands, increase our skill;
Give us courage when we falter;
Use our gift to do your will.

Christ as carpenter you labored,
Knew the joy that work can give,
Helped the fishers bring their nets in,
Taught ail people how to live;
Healed the sick, gave hope and freedom,
Fed the hungry, blessed the wine.
You who know the cost of loving,
Be for us our life's design.

In our homes, in school and office,
Hallow all the work we do,
Teaching, toiling, helping, healing,
May our lives connect with you.
Take our efforts, dreams accomplished,
Take our disappointments, pain.
Lord of life, you lived as worker,
Jesus, work through us again.[16]

SUGGESTED TUNE: HYFRYDOL
(8.7.8.7 D)

16. Marshall, "God of Work."

Worship Then Service

We worship, then we serve;
God gives, and we receive
the strength sufficient for our need—
this promise we believe.

We worship then we serve
in our community;
to open doors of trust and hope
Christ's gospel is the key.

We worship then we serve
in college, office, church
through ministry to those we meet,
support to those who search.

We worship then we serve
in workshop, clinic, school.
Each day gives opportunities
to spread Christ's loving rule.

We worship then we serve
in hospital and home
with Christ the focus of our lives,
his blessing our shalom.

To worship, then to serve:
Let this our mission be,
so all may be as one in Christ,
a world in unity.[17]

SUGGESTED TUNE: CARLISLE
(6.6.8.6)

17. Marshall, "Worship Then Service."

The Son of God, Our Christ

1. The Son of God, our Christ, the Word, the Way,
Shared human life and toiled throughout the day;
From common folk he called his friends to be
Co-workers in his sacred ministry.

2. In ev'ry test, in trials manifold,
These servants witnessed, by their faith made bold;
And with the gifts and talents which they brought,
The Church was founded and God's message taught.

3. Today, as then, Christ summons us to dare
To follow boldly and his work to share,
Declaring to the world his holy name
And showing mercy to the sick and lame.

4. In city street, in town, or on the soil,
May each serve Christ in faithful daily toil,
And in each thought and kindly word and deed,
Obey Christ's call and go where he shall lead.

5. Where'er we find our witness should be made,
Whate'er our task, the Lord will be our aid,
And we will gladly give for him our best
And find each task divinely sent and blessed.[18]

SUGGESTED TUNE: SURSUM CORDA
(10.10.10.10)

---

18. Blumenfeld, "The Son of God, Our Christ," hymn 584.

The Way, the Truth, the Life

You, Lord, the way, the truth, the life revealed;
the love at our beginning, without end.
show us that way, your truth to us make plain;
throughout our lives sustain us as our friend.

We are the workers for your harvest, Christ,
those whom you seek to cultivate the field;
empower us as we labour at our tasks
that all our efforts bring a fruitful yield.

As, through the ages, you have called to serve
men, women, chosen for their various skills,
may we continue this great work of love
with dedicated purpose, eager wills.

Until at last our earthly course is run
and we continue in a larger sphere;
new life emerging from our mortal form
as fresh shoots from the fertile soil appear.[19]

SUGGESTED TUNE: ST AGNES (LANGRAN)
(10.10.10.10)

For All with Heavy Loads to Bear

For all with heavy loads to bear,
with calls to serve, protect and care,
Whose work and life bring hard demands,
With others' welfare in their hands.
Lord, help them thrive in all they face,
Upheld by your all-loving grace.

19. Marshall, "The Way, the Truth, the Life."

Part 2: Work and Profession

For all who find their work to be
A test of their integrity,
in contracts brokered, deals secured,
In choices faced and stress endured,
Lord, grant to them the strength they need,
To follow you in word and deed.

For all who long for work and pay
To buy enough to live each day.
When skills are offered yet ignored,
And patience reaps no real reward,
Lord, where we only see despair
send purpose, hope and justice there.

For all whose work is never done,
Whose call is answered in the home,
Frustration, tiredness, love and care
Combine to build the kingdom there.
Lord, give to all whose work is love
Your inspiration from above.

In all that we will do this day
Be near us, Lord of all, we pray,
In words and actions, work and rest,
May all our moments be so blessed
That when our years and days are done
We'll find our life has just begun.[20]

SUGGESTED TUNE: MELITA (8.8.8.8.8.8)

20. Barrett, "Hymns."

O Grant Us, God, a Little Space

1. O grant us, God, a little space
from daily tasks set free.
We meet within this holy place
and find security.

2. Around us rolls the ceaseless tide
of business, toil, and care,
And scarcely can we turn aside
for one brief hour of prayer.

3. Yet this is not the only place
your presence may be found;
On daily work you shed your grace,
and blessings all around.

4. Yours are the workplace, home, and mart,
the wealth of sea and land;
The worlds of science and of art
are fashioned by your hand.

5. Work shall be prayer, if all be wrought
as you would have it done;
And prayer, by you inspired and taught,
shall then with work be one.[21]

Suggested tune: WINCHESTER OLD (8.6.8.6)

21. Ellerton, "O Grant Us, God, a Little Space," hymn 516.

9

Prayers for Particular Professions

YOUNG PEOPLE STARTING FIRST jobs. Midlife professionals changing careers. Recent retirees. Unemployed or underemployed workers. Executives and day laborers. Full-time caregivers and at-home parents. Communities include a diverse mix of workers among their members—young and old, blue collar and white collar, paid and unpaid—reflecting the many places in which God is at work in the world.

The first step to blessing work is to learn what kind of work people in your congregation do. Once you know people's stories and situations, you can learn how to speak to their needs, give thanks for their gifts, and support their callings. Getting to know people's work is an important act of ministry, whether by visiting people in their workplaces or asking explicitly about their work—and listening closely to their stories. Efforts like these can help people reframe worship not as the hour of the week to forget about work and focus on God, but to bring the fullness of their lives before God.

Once you know what work people do, imagine creative ways to acknowledge their work within worship. While the general prayers in chapter 8 gather common concerns of the community, it is equally powerful to pray for a particular type of work or profession: to name its challenges, to celebrate its members' commitments, and to bless the gifts it provides to the human community. This chapter includes prayers for a variety of workers: traditional professions (for example, law, teaching, and medicine) as well as overlooked occupations (for example, truck drivers, plumbers, and personal care attendants). According to the Bureau of Labor Statistics, the most common occupations in the United States are service oriented: retail salespeople, cashiers, food preparation workers, office clerks, registered nurses, restaurant servers, customer service representatives, manual laborers, administrative assistants, janitors, and cleaners. Prayers for these workers are included throughout the chapter to broaden the scope of the church's care and concern.

The calendar template in this chapter offers one model for recognizing a different professional group each month—through scriptural images of God that connect to the group's work, petitions to speak to their concerns, and examples of blessings for several specific professions. Another approach could be to pray for professionals when church ministers are commissioned: bless educators when you bless catechists, bless communications professionals when you bless lectors, bless musicians and artists when you bless the choir. Creating connections can help people see the work they do outside of church as holy, mirroring the service they offer within the Christian community.

When deciding to pray for a particular group, be sure to gather people from this industry or profession as part of your planning. Invite them to share their experiences in order to incorporate their voices into the prayers of the community. When are they most in need of the church's prayers and support? What do they want the church to know about their work? What part of God's work does their work reflect: healing, teaching, creating, repairing, or caring? What moments of their job bring them joy? What parts are most difficult? What is beautiful about their work? What is broken? Professionals themselves will be the ones to know the fitting moments to celebrate their work: during a busy month of their year, a season when their services are in particular demand, or a national recognition week or month honoring their vocation.

The prayers offered here are not meant to be exhaustive but illustrative—to spark your pastoral imagination. You may wish to modify these prayers and petitions to fit the context, culture, or needs of your community. (Personalized prayers for professionals are also included in the funeral resources in chapter 7.) Moments to celebrate and bless people's professional work also arise naturally within the church year and the secular calendar (part 3). Finally, the blessing ritual outlined in chapter 10 may be used with these monthly prayers.

JANUARY: HEALTH CARE

Petitions

> For all whose daily work reflects the divine work of God as healer [*physician or midwife*].
>
> For those who serve the weak and vulnerable, the sick and dying, that they might not grow weary but draw strength from Christ who cares for the least among us.
>
> For those who work within complex systems of health care, that they might see beyond bureaucracy's demands to notice the sacred presence within each patient.
>
> For professionals who suffer from burnout, especially those in the healing professions, that God may reignite the flame of their commitment and sustain their sense of calling.
>
> For those who have committed their lives to the callings of health care, including [*choose those professions that apply to your congregation*]: nurses, nursing aides, physicians, midwives, nursing home staff, emergency medical technicians, dentists, dental hygienists, chiropractors, mental health professionals, pharmacists, and veterinarians.

A Prayer for Health Care Providers

Merciful God,
your healing power is everywhere about us.
Strengthen those who work among the sick;
give them courage and confidence in everything they do.
Encourage them when their efforts seem futile
or when death prevails.
Increase their trust in your power
even to overcome death and pain and crying.
May they be thankful for every sign of health you give,
and humble before the mystery of your healing grace;
through Jesus Christ our Lord. Amen.[1]

A Blessing of Healing Hands

Yours are the hands full of experience and skill.
Yours are the hands reaching out with compassion,
Taking time to show care, swiftly taking action.

Yours are the hands gently touching your patients.
You touch families, too.
Yours are the hands that show you care.
You lift the hearts of those who suffer.
Your hands celebrate the joy of healing.
Your hands bless all they touch with the spirit of compassion.

Thank you for sharing your abundance and gifts,
For touching lives and lifting spirits.
Blessings and thanks for the many works of your hands.
May your hands bring healing to all those you touch.[2]

1. Presbyterian Church (USA), *Book of Common Worship*, 989–90.
2. Catholic Health Association of the United States, "Blessing of Healing Hands."

FEBRUARY: SCIENCE AND TECHNOLOGY

Petitions

> For all whose daily work reflects the divine work of God as creator [*or builder*].
>
> For those who create with minds or machines, technology or equipment, theories or formulas—that their work might advance our efforts to understand and live well within our world.
>
> For wisdom for all who face complicated problems and discover creative solutions; for clarity in their callings and creativity in their imaginations.
>
> For those whose work makes it possible for people to connect and communicate, for goods to be created and systems to be maintained, for lives to be saved and difficult circumstances to be improved.
>
> For those who have committed their lives to the callings of science and technology, including [*choose those professions that apply to your congregation*]: computer programmers, web developers, software engineers, information technology specialists, biomedical engineers, mechanical engineers, electrical engineers, chemical engineers, civil engineers, drafters, technicians, scientists, and researchers.

A Prayer of Thanksgiving for All Who Work in Science

> We praise you, O God, for creating humankind in your image,
> and giving all human beings a common genetic makeup
> regardless of race, gender or ethnicity;
> We are awed by the knowledge
> that there are billions of cells in our bodies and
> each one of them stores the secret of life in its DNA;
> We are amazed by scientists' use of technology
> to learn about cells, tissues and organs
> and how any changes in the gene can affect our daily lives.
> We pray for all scientists—

engineers, students, teachers, physicians, technicians—
who work diligently to unfold your holy mysteries
and ask your blessing on each one of them.
May these technological developments be used for the good of all
and to alleviate suffering from the world.
We thank you, O God,
for the wisdom and knowledge you bestow upon scientists
who work at revealing the secrets of creation.
We stand in awe and wonder at the history of the universe
and of life on this planet.
This knowledge strengthens our faith in your creative power.
We are grateful for this wonderful creation
and for being a part of your blessing.
Praise be to you, O God.[3]

A Prayer for Research and Technology

Lord God almighty,
we humbly praise you,
for you enlighten and inspire
those who by probing the powers implanted in creation
develop the work of your hands in wonderful ways.
Look with favor on your servants
who use the technology discovered by long research.
Enable them to communicate truth,
to foster love, to uphold justice and right,
and to provide employment.
Let them promote and support
that peace between peoples
which Christ the Lord brought from heaven,
for he lives and reigns with you for ever and ever.
Amen.[4]

3. White, "Thanksgiving for All."
4. International Commission on English in the Liturgy, *Book of Blessings*, 273.

MARCH: SOCIAL SERVICES

Petitions

For all whose daily work reflects the divine work of God as comforter [*advocate, healer, or guide*].

For those who bring hope and healing into the dark corners of our
world, and for those who help guide children and adults toward
well-being and fullness of life.

For those who promote the common good in schools, families,
hospitals, clinics, and treatment centers—for the strength to
be a calming presence amid trauma and tragedy and to bring
peace to people in great need.

For those who have committed their lives to the callings of social services, including [*choose those professions that apply to
your congregation*]: therapists, psychologists, social workers,
substance abuse counselors, community health workers, ministers, and those who work in social services and nonprofit
organizations.

A Prayer for Those Who Work in Social Services

Heavenly Father, whose blessed Son came not to be served but to
serve: Bless all who, following in his steps, give themselves to the
service of others; that with wisdom, patience, and courage, they
may minister in his Name to the suffering, the friendless, and the
needy; for the love of him who laid down his life for us, your Son
our Savior Jesus Christ, who lives and reigns with you and the
Holy Spirit, one God, for ever and ever. *Amen.*[5]

A Prayer for Counselors and Therapists

God of compassion,
we pray for counselors and therapists,

---

5. Episcopal Church, *Book of Common Prayer*, 260.

and all whose daily work
seeks wholeness and healing
for those they serve.

Bless their minds with wisdom:
to put knowledge into practice,
to hold each story sacred,
and to honor healthy boundaries.

Bless their ears to listen:
to what is said and unsaid,
to others' voices and to yours,
to signs of hope and healing.

Bless their eyes to see:
to recognize people as they are,
to imagine what they could become,
and to find your face in others.

Bless their mouths to speak:
to guide others toward growth,
to comfort toward wholeness,
and to shine light into darkness.

Bless their hands to serve:
to reach out in concern,
to restore strength and courage,
and to renew their commitment with each new day.

Bless their hearts to love:
to give their lives to your work of compassion,
to deepen empathy and guard against burnout,
to stand as signs of your love to all people.

We ask this in the name of the Spirit who is comforter, advocate,
and guide. Amen.

APRIL: BUSINESS

Petitions

> For all whose daily work reflects the divine work of God as servant [*or worker*].
>
> For men and women who are called to start, lead, or support businesses: for integrity in their decisions, justice in their dealings, and humility in their daily tasks.
>
> For people who work in complex corporations, that they may be guided by their faith to bring their values into the workplace and to support their community of coworkers.
>
> For those whose work is affected by forces they cannot control—the global economy, local politics, or institutional policies—that they might place their ultimate trust in God.
>
> For those who have committed their lives to the callings of business, including [*choose those professions that apply to your congregation*]: administrators, managers, office staff, administrative assistants, clerks, business owners, entrepreneurs, executives, human resources personnel, bankers, financial advisors, analysts, accountants, insurance agents, travel agents, advertising representatives, public relations professionals, salespeople, and marketers.

A Prayer for Workers in Commerce

> Almighty God, whose Son Jesus Christ in his earthly life shared our toil and hallowed our labor: Be present with your people where they work; make those who carry on the industries and commerce of this land responsive to your will; and give to us all a pride in what we do, and a just return for our labor; through Jesus Christ our Lord, who lives and reigns with you, in the unity of the Holy Spirit, one God, now and for ever. Amen.[6]

---

6. Episcopal Church, *Book of Common Prayer*, 259.

A Blessing for Business Professionals

For those who greet customers or clients—
may they find Christ in each person they meet.

For those who work with facts and figures—
may they see the faces of those whose lives they touch.

For those who work alone and those who work in teams—
may they be led by God's creative Spirit.

For those who hire and those who fire—
may they be guided by God's wisdom.

For those who respond to crisis and work under stress—
may they seek God's peace even when the stakes are high.

For those who face competition, anxiety, or uncertainty—
may they find God's comfort in what they cannot control.

For those who plan for the future and those who problem solve
today—
may their day's work be faithful and their life's legacy be long.

We ask all this in the name of God who works within us. Amen.

A Prayer for Those in Business

God of the covenant,
you give love without return,
and lavish gifts without looking for gain.
Watch over the ways of business,
so that those who buy or sell, get or lend,
may live justly and show mercy

and walk in your ways.

May profits be fair and contracts kept.

In our dealings with each other

may we display true charity;

through Jesus Christ,

who has loved us with mercy. Amen.[7]

MAY: LAW AND PUBLIC SERVICE

Petitions

For all whose daily work reflects the divine work of God as servant [*or protector*].

For those whose vocations call them into dangerous situations and for all whose work has life-or-death consequences, that they may be protected and strengthened by God each day.

For those whose professions are misunderstood or disrespected, that they might hold fast to their convictions and hold strong to God who guided them to their work.

For people who work for justice amid injustice, who work for safety amid violence, who work for peace amid war.

For those who have committed their lives to the callings of justice and public service, including [*choose those professions that apply to your congregation*]: attorneys, judges, police officers, firefighters, emergency workers, postal service workers, detectives, corrections officers, security officers, military personnel, civil servants, and government officials.

A Blessing for Those Who Serve and Protect the Common Good

God of peace and truth,

we give thanks for those among us

7. Presbyterian Church (USA), *Book of Common Worship*, 820.

who are called to work for justice,
especially those whose daily work puts them in harm's way.

Bless those who make laws
and those who defend them,
those who protect society
and those who keep it running smoothly.

Guide those who defend the innocent
and those who prosecute the guilty,
those who work behind the scenes
and those who rush in when emergencies sound the alarm.

Be with those who work within neighborhoods
and those who are called overseas,
those who work amid peace
and those who work amid violence.

May all of them—and all of us—work together
toward your vision of a world that is just, safe, and fair for all.
We ask this in Jesus's name. Amen.

A Prayer for Those Who Work in Law Enforcement

God of justice and mercy, only you know all the hurts and injustices in our community. We praise you that there are those
among us who have been called to help the community in its efforts to treat people in a just way. We ask that you be with police,
caseworkers, advocates, lawyers, judges, parole officers, prison
officials, and others who work with those who have caused harm
or are the recipients of harm.

Danger is often present in the lives of those working in law
enforcement and social services. May they know security in you.
Their decisions are often difficult and the resources too limited.
Sustain them in all circumstances. Only you can know what is
best for those whom they serve. May they receive wisdom and

compassion from you as they work. O God, we thank you for those called to this work, and we ask that they may know your presence and be aware of the prayers offered for them by this community of faith. *Amen.*[8]

A Prayer for Leaders in Public Office

Almighty God, you proclaim your truth in every age by many voices: Direct, in our time, we pray, those who speak where many listen and write what many read; that they may do their part in making the heart of this people wise, its mind sound, and its will righteous; to the honor of Jesus Christ our Lord. *Amen.*[9]

JUNE: EDUCATION

Petitions

For all whose daily work reflects the divine work of God as teacher [*or source of wisdom*].

For strength, patience, and love for all who are called to teach, and for openness, curiosity, and joy for all who are called to learn.

For educators and all professionals who live out their ideals within institutions and who fight disillusion as they try to make a difference.

For those who have committed their lives to the calling of teaching, including [*choose those professions that apply to your congregation*]: teachers, professors, principals, librarians, paraprofessionals, special education specialists, school support staff, coaches, and tutors.

8. Williams, *Worship and Daily Life*, 58.

9. Episcopal Church, *Book of Common Prayer*, 827.

A Prayer for Teachers

God of wisdom,
your Son came among us as a teacher.
Send your blessing
on all who are engaged in the work of education:
give them clearness of vision
and freshness of thought,
and enable them so to train the hearts and minds of their students
that they may grow in wisdom
and be prepared to face the challenges of life;
through Jesus Christ our Lord. Amen.[10]

A Prayer for Education

Almighty God, the fountain of all wisdom: Enlighten by your Holy Spirit those who teach and those who learn, that, rejoicing in the knowledge of your truth, they may worship you and serve you from generation to generation; through Jesus Christ our Lord, who lives and reigns with you and the Holy Spirit, one God, for ever and ever. *Amen.*[11]

JULY: PERSONAL CARE

Petitions

For all whose daily work reflects the divine work of God as comforter [*caretaker or parent*].

For those who care for "the least among us," that they will not feel isolated or overlooked, but that our community will strengthen their commitment and support their labors.

10. Evangelical Lutheran Church in America, *Evangelical Lutheran Worship*, 78.

11. Episcopal Church, *Book of Common Prayer*, 261.

For those who care for people's bodies—whether young or old, strong or weak, healthy or sick—that their sacred touch might bring God's love to those they serve.

For those who have committed their lives to the callings of caring, including [*choose those professions that apply to your congregation*]: caregivers, at-home parents, child care providers, nannies, personal care attendants, animal caretakers, fitness trainers, massage therapists, barbers, and hair stylists.

A Prayer for Those Who Raise Children

Loving God,
you care for each of us like a tender parent,
guiding and nurturing,
comforting and forgiving,
responding to our daily needs.
Bless those whose work is done behind closed doors,
beyond what society sees:
for those who comfort babies, teach toddlers, raise children, or parent teenagers;
for those who work round the clock, day and night;
for those who cook, clean, feed, bathe, drive, teach, listen, and love.
May they know their work is worthy, even when it is unpaid.
May they know their calling matters, even when it is unnoticed.
May they know their vocation is holy, even when it is humbling.
We ask that you guide these adults, and the children in their lives,
as they call them into deeper faith, greater wisdom, and stronger love.
Amen.

A Prayer for Those Who Give Care

Lover of souls,
we bless your Holy Name
for all who are called to mediate your grace
to those who are sick or infirm.
Sustain them by your Holy Spirit,
that they may bring your loving-kindness
to those in pain, fear, and confusion;
that in bearing one another's burdens
they may follow the example of our Savior Jesus Christ.
Amen.[12]

A Prayer for Those Who Bring Healing

May you walk among the people you serve,
May you be one with them.
May others see your care,
May they catch your gift.

May your soul be nourished by the work you do,
The service you perform.
May your heart be lifted in the struggles you endure.

May you know the mission
In your very bones.
May it challenge you and sustain you.

May you risk all that is secure for you,
That you may reach all that is central to you
And find goodness there.
May courage befriend you,

12. Episcopal Church, *Enriching Our Worship*, 93.

Integrity sustain you,
Hope call you forward.

May you walk on the water of faith
Toward the One who calls us all.

Amen.[13]

AUGUST: MANUFACTURING AND CONSTRUCTION

Petitions

For all whose daily work reflects the divine work of God as builder [*creator or architect*].

For those who repair what is broken, maintain what is working, and construct what needs to be built, that we may recognize the good they bring to our community.

For those who turn ideas into reality by the work of their hands and the sweat of their brows.

For those who work outdoors and those who work in harm's way: for protection from injury, safety on the job site, and rest after a hard day's work.

For those who have committed their lives to the calling of building, including [*choose those professions that apply to your congregation*]: architects, laborers, electricians, plumbers, carpenters, landscapers, landscape architects, mechanics, service technicians, factory workers, equipment operators, and highway workers.

A Prayer for Laborers

Christ who was carpenter and craftsman,
you knew the value of a hard day's work.

13. Catholic Health Association of the United States, "Blessing for Health Care Leaders."

Bless all who labor with their hands—
with tools or machines,
in factories or shops,
on highways or in homes.

As their efforts build up our communities,
guide their work and bless their rest
that the fruits of their labors
might proclaim the value of their callings
and celebrate the quality of a job well done.
We ask this in your name. Amen.

A Prayer for Those Who Build

O God, the builder of all things,
you have placed on us the obligation of toil.
Grant that the work we begin
may serve to better our lives
and through your goodness contribute
to the spread of the kingdom of Christ,
who lives and reigns with you and the Holy Spirit,
one God, for ever and ever.
Amen.[14]

SEPTEMBER: TRANSPORTATION INDUSTRY

Petitions

For all whose daily work reflects the divine work of God as companion for travelers [*or guide*].

---

14. International Commission on English in the Liturgy, *Book of Blessings*, 246.

For those who transport goods and people; for those who work to maintain the means of transportation; and for all who keep our communities running day and night.

For those who work on roads and rails, in airports and harbors, in cities and rural areas, that wherever the people of God go, they may know the presence of God.

For those who have committed their lives to the calling of transportation, including [*choose those professions that apply to your congregation*]: truck drivers, taxi drivers, bus drivers, delivery workers, pilots, flight attendants, baggage handlers, railroad workers, and sailors.

A Prayer for Drivers and Travelers

Christ, you are our beginning and our ending,
our Alpha and Omega.
Bless all those who leave home to travel for their work:
those who deliver goods from factory to store,
those who take people from one town to the next,
those who travel the world by plane, ship, or train.
Watch over their comings and goings,
and keep them safe across the miles,
as they answer a call that leads far from home.
As their work keeps our lives running,
may our prayers go with them always:
in their labors and their travels, whether near or far.
We ask this in your name,
Amen.

A Prayer for Those Who Work in Transportation

Christ, the Son of God,
came into the world to gather those who were scattered.

Whatever contributes to bringing us closer together
therefore is in accord with God's plan.
Thus those who are separated from each other
by mountains, oceans, or great distances
are brought nearer to each other
whenever new highways are built
or other means of transportation developed.

Let us, then, call on God
to bless those who have worked on this project
and to protect with his gracious help
those who will make use of it.[15]

OCTOBER: ARTS AND COMMUNICATIONS

Petitions

For all whose daily work reflects the divine work of God as artist
[*creator or potter*].

For those who enrich others' lives through the arts, opening eyes
and ears and hearts to see God's presence in the world.

For those whose work is communication, that they may be inspired
by God's word to write and speak what is good, beautiful, and
true.

For those who have committed their lives to the calling of creating, including [*choose those professions that apply to your congregation*]: artists, graphic designers, actors, interior designers,
florists, musicians, writers, editors, translators, news reporters,
producers, and communications staff.

15. Ibid., 285.

Part 2: Work and Profession

A Prayer for Artists and Musicians

God of life,
you filled the world with beauty.
Thank you for artists who see clearly,
who with trained skill
can paint, shape, or sing your truth to us.
Keep them attentive
and ready to applaud the wonder of your works,
finding in the world signs of the love
revealed in Jesus Christ our Lord. Amen.[16]

A Prayer for Those Who Create

Bless the creators, O God of creation,
who by their gifts make the world
a more joyful and beautiful realm.
Through their labors
they teach us to see more clearly
the truth around us.
In their inspiration
they call forth wonder and awe
in our own living.
In their hope and vision
they remind us
that life is holy.
Bless all who create in your image,
O God of creation.
Pour your Spirit upon them
that their hearts may sing
and their words be fulfilling;
in the name of Christ, we pray.
Amen.[17]

16. Lutheran Church in America, *Lutheran Book of Worship*, 110.
17. Anderson, *Prayers of Our Hearts*, 65.

A Prayer for Writers and Communicators

God of the word,
you spoke and all things came into being.
Bless all who work with words—
who write, speak, read,
edit, report, and translate.

Guide their minds with your wisdom.
Inspire the work of their hands.
Let your beauty and truth
speak through the words they use,
the ideas they shape,
and the lives they touch.

May all of us who write, read, speak, or listen each day
be mindful of the power of words—
to build up or tear down,
to create or destroy,
to heal or to wound,
to unite or to divide.

Bless those whom you call to work through words:
to shine light into darkness,
to share what is hidden,
to make known what is true.

We ask this in the name of Jesus your Son,
the Word who was from the beginning.
Amen.

NOVEMBER: CUSTOMER SERVICE

Petitions

> For all whose daily work reflects the divine work of God as laborer [*servant, gardener, farmer, or host*].
>
> For all who labor under difficult conditions: for those who work late hours, multiple jobs, or extra shifts; for those who work in hot, cold, or unsafe conditions; for those who must serve each customer whether kind or harsh, gentle or impatient, demanding or forgiving.
>
> For those who serve and care for others by their daily work, that they might be served and cared for in turn.
>
> For those who have committed their lives to the calling of service, including [*choose those professions that apply to your congregation*]: cooks, restaurant servers, dishwashers, bakers, farmers, agricultural workers, farm laborers, fishermen, food production workers, factory workers, janitors, housekeepers, cleaners, hotel staff, and customer service representatives.

A Prayer for Those Who Serve with Their Hands

> God whose hands bring hope and healing,
> we pray for all who work with their hands:
> those who scrub, sweep, and wash;
> who plant, weed, and pick;
> who fish, catch, and clean;
> who cook, bake, and serve;
> who box, stack, and shelve.
> May their hands bring blessing to those they serve.
> May our hands receive their work with gratitude.
> We raise our hands to you in praise. Amen.

A Prayer for Customer Service Representatives

God of goodness, you made us in your image.
When we strive to love, we reflect your love to others.

Today we pray for those who work in customer service,
who spend their days helping, listening, and serving.

Like you, may they be slow to anger and rich in kindness.
Like you, may they offer compassion and patience.
Like you, may they be forgiving and fair.
Like you, may their words be full of truth.
Like you, may they be known by their mercy.

God of love, each day we seek each other's help—
in the store, at the counter,
on the phone, through the screen.
May we give thanks to all
who give time and energy to serve us.
And may we remember our common calling to serve one another.
We ask all this in your name. Amen.

DECEMBER: RETAIL

Petitions

For all whose daily work reflects the divine work of God as servant [*or leader*].

For all who spend their days serving others, helping them get the goods and services they need to do their own work.

For those who seek to bring their faith into each encounter in their workplace, store, or business, no matter how small or big, slow or rushed, positive or negative.

For those who have committed their lives to the calling of business and sales, including [*choose those professions that apply to your congregation*]: salespeople, cashiers, sales supervisors, managers, and store owners.

A Prayer for Retail Workers

When the hours are late, give us hope.
When the tasks are hard, give us strength.
When the customers are impatient, give us peace.
When the schedule is demanding, give us calm.
When the body is tired, give us rest.

When the goals are met, give us joy.
When the energy runs high, give us thanks.
When the coworkers are kind, give us love.
When the need is real, give us faith.
When the day is good, give us peace.

A Prayer for Those in Sales and Commerce

God, we thank you that there are those you have called to serve through commerce. Through the intricate matters that they must handle, help them to remain faithful to your love. May they see each customer as one of your children.

Help them to ask the difficult questions that need to be asked. Help them to be dissatisfied with quick gain over long-needed results. Guide them to use resources wisely. Strengthen their resolve to use their gifts in service to you and others. May they help their coworkers find joy in service. We thank you for their call to this work, and we ask that they may be aware of your presence and be strengthened by the prayers given for them by this community of faith. *Amen.*[18]

18. Williams, *Worship and Daily Life*, 59.

10

A Rite of Blessing for Workers

PRAYING OVER PEOPLE'S WORK is a powerful witness to the church's belief that people are created in the image of God who is at work in the world. One way to affirm the holiness of work—and that many people consider their occupation or profession to be a calling—is to offer what some Christian traditions call a "commissioning service" or an "affirmation of Christian vocation," which is a ritual of blessing for particular professions. People may forget almost every sermon they hear, but they will never forget coming forward to be prayed over by their community. Professionals long to hear a good word spoken about their work, and Christians from all walks of life need to be reminded that they need not be ministers or missionaries to be called by God. Even workers who do not consider their job a vocation can be encouraged by having their work blessed and hearing how God could be at work through their job or in their workplace.

The following Rite of Blessing for particular professions may be used within Sunday worship to offer regular blessings of people's work. The rite is short and adaptable so that it can be a realistic addition to your congregation's order of worship. If your ministry takes place outside the congregational setting, you may wish to modify the blessing; for example, to bless an individual receiving spiritual direction; to bless college students by majors in campus ministry; or to bless a mixed group of professionals as part of a retreat.

To prepare for the rite, announce the blessing several weeks in advance from the pulpit, church bulletin, or newsletter. Offer a list of the professionals who will be included in the blessing. Invite people to bring in a symbol or tool of their trade. You may also wish to ask several parishioners who are members of this profession to write a short description of how they experience God's call to this profession or within their daily work. These "calling stories" could be shared in the church bulletin, included in your sermon, or adapted for a prayer of petition. Professionals' own witness about the connections between their faith and their work offer powerful testimonies for the community to hear.

Several additional rites of blessings are included at the end of the chapter to illustrate the variety of ways in which a regular prayer for workers can be incorporated into your congregation's worship. Depending on your church's order of worship, you may include a blessing for workers at the beginning of the service, after the sermon, or before the final blessing. You could also invite members of the profession to be involved in other parts of the service to include their gifts and highlight their presence within the community.

ORDER OF THE RITE OF BLESSING FOR WORKERS

Gathering

Begin by asking professionals from the particular group to stand or come forward if they are able. Offer a word of welcome and a brief introduction about why your community has chosen to bless this particular profession today. You may wish to take a moment of silence before you begin and invite the congregation to reflect on those whose work has touched their lives this week, as a way to begin your prayer to God who works through our work.

God who is the caller of our lives,
we come before you today
to celebrate those among us who work as [*specify profession*].
We believe that they are called by you,

that they are called through others,
that they are called for service,
and that they are called to our community.
Today we gather their gifts, their needs, and their concerns
and ask you to sustain them in their callings.
May they know their work is worthy;
may they know that they are loved.

Offering

Bring forward or lift up tools of the trade. You may wish to prepare in advance a space in the sanctuary with several symbols of the profession in order to encourage people to add their own. Or you can invite the workers being honored to write down one way they have served God through their work or felt God calling them to work. They can bring forward their slips of paper and place them in a basket as another symbolic offering.

God of work and workers,
Bless these objects and symbols of this profession,
and all whom these men and women help, touch, or serve.
May they always know that you are with them in their daily labors,
that you work through their minds, hearts, and hands.

Thanksgiving

Lift up the gifts of this profession to the community. As you give thanks for the members of this profession and how they reflect God to others, you may wish to invite the congregation to remember professionals from this industry who have touched their lives by their service—recently or in the past. This prayer of thanksgiving could be read by others (for example, friends, family, or spouses of the professionals being blessed).

God of goodness,
we give thanks for this profession,
for how its work touches our lives
and serves the common good.
We give thanks for the gifts of these professionals,
their talents, skills, capacities, and concerns.
Most of all, we give thanks for their service to those in need.
May their work reflect your love for us,
and may their lives respond to your call.

Confessing

Ask for the community's support and prayers for the struggles and challenges faced by this profession. This prayer could be read by a representative from the profession being blessed, as a prophetic witness to all workers to seek forgiveness for the times they have failed to live up to God's hopes for their callings.

God of mercy,
we ask you to look with compassion
upon these women and men who seek to do your will.
Forgive their sins, their failings and temptations—
the times they choose their way and not your own,
the moments they lose hope or doubt your love,
the frustrations or fears that cloud their vision.
Call them to return to you again
and strengthen their resolve to do their work
with generous and humble hearts.

Interceding

Gather the particular concerns of the workers being blessed. This can be a powerful moment to invite the professionals themselves to take part in the Rite of Blessing, by reading the prayers of petitions or offering their own to include in the list below. Use a responsive refrain common to your congregation's worship (for example, Lord, hear our prayer).

For the needs of these professionals, especially [*insert particular need here*].

For those who are preparing to become [*professionals*].

For those who have retired from [*profession*].

For those not present among us who are called to be [*professionals*].

For those who have died who gave their lives to this work.

For all those whose daily work connects with the workers being blessed today, especially for . . .

Blessing

End with a promise of the community's prayers and support. You may choose to bless people's hands or have the congregation stretch out their hands to bless their fellow members. You could also choose to close the rite by singing the doxology or praying the Our Father together as a sign of the community's shared Christian calling.

God of our callings,

We ask you to bless these men and women gathered here today.

Fill them with your strength,

Guide them with your love.

Let them know of our prayers and support for their daily work.

Lead all of us to work together

toward your vision of flourishing for creation.

We ask that you bless each one of us in our labors,

and send us forth to serve in your name.

(Stretch out your hands in blessing or bless the hands of each person in turn.)

May God bless you and the work of your hands,

now and forever.

Amen.

OTHER RITES OF BLESSING FOR WORK

A Blessing of the Tools of a Profession

O God,
the fullness of blessing comes down from you,
to you our prayers of blessing rise up.
In your kindness protect your servants,
who stand before you devout and faithful,
bearing the tools of their trade.

Grant that their hard work may contribute
to the perfecting of your creation
and provide a decent life for themselves and their families.
Help them to strive for a better society
and to praise and glorify your holy name always.

We ask this through Christ our Lord.

Amen.[1]

Affirmation of Christian Vocation

Within the sending rite of the service, this affirmation may be made by individuals or groups, and may be introduced by a description of the area of service to be affirmed. Or the affirmation may be made by the whole assembly.

The presiding minister addresses those affirming Christian vocation.

[*Sisters and brothers]/[name/s],* both your work and your rest are in God. Will you endeavor to pattern your life on the Lord Jesus Christ, in gratitude to God and in service to others, at morning and evening, at work and at play, all the days of your life?

Response: I will, and I ask God to help me.

1. International Commission on English in the Liturgy, *Book of Blessings,* 321.

The presiding minister continues.

Almighty God, by the power of the Spirit you have knit these your servants into the one body of your Son, Jesus Christ. Look with favor upon them in their commitment to serve in Christ's name. Give them courage, patience, and vision; and strengthen us all in our Christian vocation of witness to the world and of service to others; through Jesus Christ our Lord. Amen.

The service concludes with the blessing and dismissal.[2]

A Litany of Dedication

Liturgist: While Moses was tending sheep on a mountainside, the Lord appeared to him in a burning bush and called out to him, saying, "Take off your sandals, for the place where you are standing is holy ground." Jesus taught us that all ground is holy: all of life for our Master is a sacrament to be dedicated fully to God. Each of us is the temple of the Holy Spirit. We are on holy ground in our work as teachers, lawyers, volunteers, doctors, parents, secretaries, students, business owners, construction workers, and every other vocation God has given us. Today we affirm before God and one another that our work and our worship are interwoven, our work growing out of worship and our worship growing out of work.

Teacher: As teachers, let our classrooms be places where your light and your truth shine in all learning, and where we celebrate and nurture the varied gifts and abilities of each student.

Student: As students, let our minds, our talents, and our character be shaped more and more in your image as we learn to use our gifts in the service of your kingdom.

Worker: In the workplace, may mutual respect govern our relationships, and integrity govern our contracts and finances, as we produce useful goods and services.

2. Evangelical Lutheran Church in America, *Evangelical Lutheran Worship*, 84.

Caregiver: As caregivers of children and family, the sick and the aged, may we remember the example of Jesus as he washed the feet of his disciples, and treat each person as one who bears God's image.

Scientist, writer, or artist: As scientists, writers, and artists, may your Spirit inspire and govern the work of our minds, and transform the professions in which we work.

Retiree: As those retired from many years of work, may we enjoy the gift of rest, encourage one another, pray for the church, and mentor the next generation.

Congregation: In all our daily labors, even amidst dull routine or frustrating demands, may we hear the call to serve the Lord.

Liturgist: Take a few moments now to pray and meditate on your daily work—its joys, challenges, worries, and relationships— and how these might be more fully dedicated to God in the coming year.

Time of silent meditation and prayer
Amen.[3]

3. Haarsma, "People Had a Mind to Work," 38.

PART 3

A Year of Blessing

For everything there is a season, and a time for every matter under heaven:

a time to be born, and a time to die;

a time to plant, and a time to pluck up what is planted;

a time to kill, and a time to heal;

a time to break down, and a time to build up;

a time to weep, and a time to laugh;

a time to mourn, and a time to dance.

—ECCL 3:1–4

THE RHYTHMS OF BOTH the church year and the cultural calendar offer bountiful opportunities for ministers to pray and preach about vocation. Since preaching aims to connect the stories of Scripture with the stories of people's lives today, the final section in this book offers practical, pastoral ideas for sermon preparation by looking at seasons and feasts through the lens of vocation. Chapter 11 (Celebrations of the Calendar Year) and chapter 12 (Seasons of the Church Year) also provide helpful resources for those engaged in retreat work, religious education, and ministry in nontraditional settings. As communities prepare, remember, and celebrate together, they are shaped by the changing of their callings over time.

11

Celebrations of the Calendar Year

CULTURAL HOLIDAYS CAN OFFER preaching opportunities to explore the diversity of callings throughout the year. This chapter gives several examples from each calendar season as ways to give commonly celebrated holidays a vocational twist and inspire you to think creatively about the dates that hold particular importance for your community. Each of these secular feasts contains elements that can be celebrated by the church and elements that may need to be challenged or questioned. Examining popular holidays through the lens of vocation allows for a healthy approach—one that acknowledges the positive meaning of the celebration but does not acquiesce to problematic aspects of the holiday. What and who are we called to be, as individuals and as communities, through our shared celebrations?

FALL

Halloween

Children's favorite fall holiday celebrates the power of possibility. Beyond costumes and candy lies the delight of pretending to be someone or something else for a night. Part of the calling of children and teenagers is to try on possible selves and dream of the people they may become. What children feel called to be matters—not only for their vocations within childhood but also for their callings in adulthood. Halloween is also a communal holiday. Unlike other feasts celebrated by families at home, our Halloween practices involve leaving home. Children and parents venture out into neighborhoods, apartment hallways, streets, and sidewalks— a small step that symbolizes the ways in which they go out into the world together, even in the dark of an autumn evening, in search of something good together. While some churches have been wary of the implications of celebrating Halloween, the opportunity to focus on the imaginative and joyful aspects of this holiday for children can be a place to connect with the concept of calling.

Veterans Day

November 11 is a day to remember the service of all who have served in the United States Armed Forces. Many people feel called to serve in the military, and the challenges and complexities of this work remind us that vocation entails sacrifice. Yet congregations can find themselves caught between the desire to support its members' service and the Christian call to work for peace. Similar questions can arise with September 11. Praying for people who have served in the military while also praying for peace can allow the community to acknowledge, rather than avoid, both sides of a complex calling. This day also serves to remind the country about its responsibility to care for returning veterans: a shared calling not to forget those who have suffered.

Thanksgiving

Even though Thanksgiving is not an explicitly Christian holiday, it can feel like a faith-filled celebration, resonant with regular rhythms of worship in which we gather around the table, give thanks, and break bread. Gratitude is part of every response to a call from God. However, Thanksgiving's traditional practice of returning home to share a meal as a family cannot distract Christians from the truth that they are called to care for those outside their family. Vocation is not only about us and ours. If Thanksgiving is understood as a eucharistic feast (according to the Greek origins of the word, meaning "to give thanks"), then the meaning of the holiday is broadened. How can it become a feast where hunger meets nourishment, as at the communion table? Thanksgiving offers a natural moment for churches to organize food drives or prepare holiday dinners for the hungry in the community—an example of a congregation's calling. Radical welcome is part of the prophetic witness that each Christian is called to work toward for the reign of God, in which all enjoy a share in God's abundance.

WINTER

New Year's Day

The first day of a new year feels like a fresh start, turning a clean page on the calendar. Beginnings are often full of hope, and vocation can feel easier when it is fresh and new, too: a marriage in its honeymoon phase, a new job yet-unmarred by office politics, or a sweet baby rather than a surly teenager. But responding to a new calling can also feel terrified: flinging ourselves into the unknown of a career change, leaving behind an unhealthy relationship, or moving away from a toxic environment. When framed in terms of our relationship with God as the caller of our lives, New Year's invites us to hope and to trust. We can receive the new year as a gift, welcoming the potential it holds and remembering God's loving care.

Martin Luther King Jr. Day

The life and work of Dr. King raises important questions regarding the concept of vocation. What part are we called to play—as individuals and as communities—in working toward justice? How are callings shaped by racial, ethnic, and religious identity? What will be the legacy of our own vocation? Dr. King's birthday is an occasion to pray for those who work for racial justice and equality within our communities, as well as an invitation to consider how God calls us through the world's needs in our particular time and place.

Valentine's Day

Beyond the greeting cards, boxes of chocolate, and bouquets of roses, people are created for relationship and called to love. This sacred love is lived out in our relationships and our daily work; it is not limited to those we choose but needed by all those whom God calls us to serve. Valentine's Day can be a creative moment to preach about the role of love in guiding and shaping our vocations. Who has shaped us by their love? Where and whom are we called to love more deeply? How can our faith community become a clearer reflection of God's loving mercy? Valentine's Day is also a moment to pray for those who feel unloved or forgotten within our own community. As with any secular holiday, the church can affirm the positive elements (a celebration of love), resist the negative aspects (commercialization or alienation), and offer an alternative interpretation (the Christian call to love of neighbor that transcends affection and affiliation).

Presidents' Day

Taking time to remember those who have led our country places public leadership within the context of vocation and offers an opportunity to explore the Christian call to service. This holiday can be a time to pray for those in positions of power and authority, whether in our communities, churches, or country. We are connected within the web of callings, and it matters that each of us approaches our decision making with wisdom and our daily work with humility.

SPRING

Earth Day

The call to be a faithful steward is part of Christian discipleship in all areas of life. Earth Day reminds us that we are called to be stewards of creation—the earth and all its creatures. As humans we are part of creation and must also tend to its care. Furthermore, the physical world is the concrete context for our callings. Our vocations happen in place, and if we do not each take care of the earth and environment, all of creation suffers. The God of all creation calls us into relationship with the complex interdependence of all forms of life that call the earth home.

Mother's Day

Mother's Day can be a beautiful moment to celebrate the multiple and diverse ways that women care for others as mothers, stepmothers, grandmothers, and godmothers and through other significant relationships. However, this day can also be painful: for those struggling with infertility, miscarriage, or the loss of a child; for those who never knew their mother or had a difficult relationship with their mother; or for those whose mother has died. Mother's Day can therefore be an important time to acknowledge the complicated nature of our callings. Some vocations are harder than expected, some are heavy with heartache, and some callings go unfulfilled. The church can offer healing and comfort by widening its attention and prayer to include the complex facets of this holiday.

Memorial Day

While Veterans Day honors all who have served in the armed forces, Memorial Day is set aside to remember those who have died in the service of their country—what is often referred to as the "ultimate sacrifice." This day is for the living, too: the loved ones who grieve their beloved dead and the country that knows it must recognize the cost of war. Memorial Day has become well known as the unofficial start to summer—a paradox that an observance about endings is considered a beginning to summer's season of fun. This day set aside for collective remembering can surface questions that connect past and present. What is the role of memory in shaping our vocations? How can looking back help us to look forward? Who are those whose sacrifices—even in giving their own lives—have allowed us to follow our callings today?

SUMMER

Father's Day

Preaching about parenting as a vocation can offer a prophetic alternative to impoverished notions of paternity. What does it mean to be called to be a father? What happens when this vocation is embraced and when it is rejected? As with Mother's Day, Father's Day can be difficult for many people: those who wanted to become fathers but did not; those whose fathers hurt them; those who never knew their fathers; those who are grieving their fathers. But the complexity of the holiday only reinforces the power of using vocation as a lens to offer a different perspective. Churches can celebrate fathers—dads, stepdads, grandfathers, godfathers, and many others—while still reaching out to those whose own callings have suffered from the absence of a caring father figure.

Independence Day

Beyond flying the flag or wearing red, white, and blue, what does it mean to be a citizen of the United States? What impact does our homeland have on our vocation? How do people who are not citizens have a place in our communities? The Fourth of July tends toward loud and proud showcases of patriotism, but quieter conversations and deeper questions are meaningful, too. On a day dedicated to independence, we can consider the role of freedom in our callings. A vocation cannot be forced or imposed on another.

Among the conditions that allow callings to flourish are freedom from oppression and freedom of expression. Even God allows each person the free will to accept or reject any call that is offered. So considering our own choices within the context of calling can bring a grounded perspective to the abstract concept of freedom. The call to work together for the common good is a vocation all citizens share, transcending their political divides.

Labor Day

Made in the image of God who is always at work in the world, we are each called to work within the context of our lives, needs, gifts, abilities, and responsibilities. Labor Day calls us back to a more just view of work and vocation oriented toward the common good. As part of the interdependent web of vocations, we are also called to work toward justice, safety, opportunity, and resources for the work of others as well. Churches can celebrate this truth on Labor Day: that we depend on the work of others and we are called to serve them in return.

12

Seasons of the Church Year

SCRIPTURAL THEMES CAN OFFER clear opportunities to preach on vocation: the call stories of Old and New Testament figures, Jesus's teachings on discipleship, Gospel themes of Christian service and agapic love, and Pauline reflections on the nature of community, mission, and charism. But natural points of convergence between vocation and other Christian doctrines or disciplines also arise from the seasons of the church year.

This chapter offers a calendar of preaching ideas drawing from seasonal themes that connect with calling. Some churches within the Christian traditions follow a highly formalized liturgical year, while others have a more flexible and open approach to their worship. To evoke your own creative thinking of how to preach about vocation, I offer several thematic examples under seasons of the church year commonly celebrated in the Revised Common Lectionary and the Roman Catholic Lectionary (including Christian feasts commonly celebrated in Free Church traditions). My hope is for these examples to stimulate your own thinking about how theological concepts related to calling can be explored throughout the year.

ORDINARY TIME

Callings Are Mostly Ordinary

Ordinary time is where we spend most of our lives, working and loving in the day to day. While this might seem mundane and unexceptional, Jesus's own experience was largely the same: the majority of his life was never mentioned in the Gospels. But his decades of regular work and ordinary time were important for the living out of his calling—and not only for what he would become in the future (his years of ministry and his passion, death, and resurrection). Jesus was also following God's call during the ordinary years, too: in his relationships with his family, friends, and neighbors; in his daily work alongside Joseph as a carpenter; and in the deepening of his prayer life. The Gospel stories proclaimed during ordinary time often involve both extraordinary miracles and everyday conversations between Jesus and his followers. Thinking about all the unremarkable time he spent with his disciples can broaden our expectations about vocation to include the regular routines of our own lives.

Sabbath Offers Rhythms of Work and Rest

Most of the Sundays we spend together as a congregation are ordinary: we worship together in between running kids to sports practice, visiting relatives in the nursing home, doing weekend chores or errands. These everyday rhythms are holy, too, because they are vocational. We are called not only to work but also to worship, to rest, and to play—all the stuff of sabbath. Rather than viewing the weekend as time off from our vocations, the practice of sabbath encourages an integrated, embodied view of callings as who we are, how we live, and what we do—seven days a week. Scripture passages that reference the ancient Israelites' beliefs about sabbath can open up contemporary conversations about structuring our personal and professional schedules as a spiritual discipline.

Vocation and Kairos

Our attitudes toward time as it relates to our work or relationships can have a dramatic impact on our vocations. People often speak of making time, using time, wasting time, or wanting more time. Yet we are all given the same number of hours in each day. As seen in the New Testament, the ancient Greeks distinguished between *kairos* (eternal time) and *chronos* (chronological time). Our challenge as Christians is to let God's *kairos* break into our *chronos*, transforming our ordinary work into sacred service. Rather than pitting *kairos* and *chronos* against each other, vocation invites us to hold the two in dynamic, creative tension—to see ordinary time as fertile ground for God's work in and through us.

ADVENT

Preparation Is Part of Vocation

We err when we assume that vocations are something fully formed, handed down from God in their completeness, and confined to the major decisions of adulthood. Vocation is our fundamental relationship with God, which began at the moment of our creation and is constantly evolving and deepening. So all our preparations for what lies ahead of us—whether we are children at play, students in school, or retirees in transition—is part of our vocation. Advent's season of preparation for Christmas reminds us of this truth: as the people of God awaited the birth of a savior, they were already called into faithful giving of their lives. As when expectant parents prepare for the arrival of their child, they are already living into their new calling, transforming their relationship with each other, with God, and with the wider world, even as they are still on the side of possibility, planning, and preparation.

Vocations Mean Waiting

The basic nature of vocation implies waiting in between: first God calls, then we respond. How do we live in the waiting time? What does discernment mean in a culture that has forgotten the value of quiet, patience, and prayer? Every vocation involves some waiting, whether a decision about what work to do, where to live, how to cope with suffering, or whom to share our lives with. Once we begin to sense the inner urging of a call, we must wait for its full expression while we plan and prepare. So too does Advent involve patient waiting before the climax of Christmas. We are called to wait, and waiting changes us, too. Advent's anticipatory nature reminds us that we are often counting down to the big moments in our lives (like vocational turning points), but we are also living out our vocations all along.

Vocation beyond Death

What does heaven mean for our callings here and now? Beliefs about the soul, salvation, and the afterlife matter deeply for our vocations today. Why work or live as a response to God's call if earthly existence is the end limit of our lives? That we are made for reunion with God and long for the completeness of this joy means that vocations have an eschatological aspect. We are already and not yet; we are now and we are still becoming. Advent's Scripture readings speak of Jesus's return at the end of the age as well as his coming as the Christ child. This dual nature of Advent's preparation and anticipation reminds us that the flawed realities of our callings—shared with imperfect people, housed in flawed institutions, and carried out by our own sinful selves—is not a shameful failing but the incomplete nature of anything earthly compared to the fullness of eternity.

CHRISTMAS

Culture Can Contort Callings

Our callings today are lived out within a consumerist culture. Consumption, shopping, and buying are nearly impossible to resist or avoid. From Black Friday through the holiday "shopping season," December has become the most commercially saturated month on the calendar. Making intentional decisions to step back from the frenzy, to simplify our celebrations and traditions, and to spend time in silence and quiet during the darkest month of the year in the Northern Hemisphere can reclaim Christmas as a holy moment, not a wholly exhausting endeavor. Communities that stake this countercultural stance can be a welcome haven for those overwhelmed by the financial pressures, emotional intensity, and superficial distractions of society's secularized version of a central Christian feast.

Gifts Are for Others

In a season laser-focused on shopping, it can be easy to forget the real meaning of gifts. Paul's notion of *charism* as a gift given by God for the good of the community reminds us that the most important gifts are not ours to keep. They are God's power and Spirit moving through us for the flourishing of the common good. Cultivating gratitude for what we are given and generosity for what we are called to share is an essential vocational practice, reminding us that Christian love is always agapic.

Vocation in the Flesh

What does the incarnation mean for our callings? Christmas celebrates the in-breaking of God entering the world in a particular and powerful way—through the Christ child. Incarnation is intimately linked to vocation, because it reminds us that our relationship with God is grounded in the concrete time and place where we find ourselves as physical beings. We are not merely spiritual beings, communing with the divine. Our callings are messy, earthly, bodily realities. Like a baby born into a dirty, noisy, smelly stable, God comes into our lives today in surprising and often embodied ways.

EPIPHANY OR ORDINARY TIME

Will Providence Provide?

The idea that God has a secret, detailed blueprint for each life still lingers in many people's view of vocation. Rather than being comforted, people are anxious that they might have missed or messed up God's plan for their life. Contemporary theological understandings have shifted to embrace a broader view of providence: that God sustains all of creation and guides people toward God's purposes in the world, drawing all life into the heart of the Trinity. Epiphany can offer a chance to unpack the concept of providence in relation to vocation. The definition of *epiphany* as a moment of sudden insight relates to the revelation of Jesus's incarnation to the magi. But what the church celebrates on a single feast day would have been a long and arduous journey as they followed the star. Their model of trust, commitment, and sacrifice for what they sought connects Epiphany with our callings today. Like the wise magi, we can learn to let ourselves be led—not necessarily by stars seen in the night sky, but by invitations placed in our path, people who guide us, and signs of God's presence that sustain us.

Live in the In-between

Between the intensity of Christmas and Easter is down time, not only a welcome lull in the church calendar between high seasons but also a pause in personal preparations for "the next big thing." The church season of Epiphany or Ordinary Time before Lent begins can serve as an important reminder that we are called to the present moment. Even if today is ordinary and uneventful, it is still potent with the presence of God. By extension, vocation involves both the major decisions and the daily activities of our lives. The living out of our callings is as important as the discernment that brought us there. So too does Ordinary Time invite us to live into quiet moments of epiphany where we deepen our understanding of where God is calling us—both now and next.

Who Is God and Who Are We?

The deepest questions of our lives form the foundational relationship of faith, which is our calling. The season between the celebrations of incarnation (Christmas) and resurrection (Easter) can be seen as a time of invitation to enter into these vocational questions. Thinking about what makes us human and what makes God divine may seem on the surface to be an esoteric theological pursuit. But its implications are immediate and practical. If God is good, what does it mean when we encounter suffering? If we have free will, what control does God have over our lives? Questions without easy answers are—despite our desire for instant gratification—the heart of vocation. While we long for clarity in our callings, much of what makes for growth in our maturity is the ability to live with mystery. Whether your community celebrates this season as Epiphany or Ordinary Time, the potential is ripe for exploring big questions together.

LENT

To Dust We Shall Return

The beginning of Lent, often celebrated as Ash Wednesday, stands as a stark reminder of our own mortality. From dust we have come, and to dust we shall return. Lent is a season of prayer and penance, inviting us to seek humility as we do the work that God invites us to do and become the people God asks us to be. This reminder of our own humanity and sinfulness sets our callings to service, work, and relationships in right relationship with God. We are not in control; we cannot live beyond our own limits; but we can still do much good for the people and places to whom we are sent. And ultimately, the call to die will come for each of us—the ultimate call beyond, into the heart and life of God that is the mystery of heaven. Remembering our own mortality while we are still alive is a part of living into our vocations. Lent allows us to take on this perspective as a vocational practice.

We Are Called to Forgive

Forgiveness has an important place in vocation. If we see our vocation as a constant conversion, turning back to God again and again, we can deepen the relationship that will sustain us through the challenges and disillusions that come with callings. Not only do we need to seek God's forgiveness when we choose selfishness over love, but we also need to forgive ourselves the shortcomings and failures that inevitably arise, even as we seek to live faithfully. Lent's focus on turning back to God—through the three traditional practices of prayer, fasting, and almsgiving—reminds us of the powerful relationship between confession and conversion. When we tell the truth about how we struggle, this conversation (with God, ourselves, or each other) can lead to changed perspective and deeper commitment. We re-member ourselves back into the body of Christ as we go through Lent, and this invitation into honesty and humility can deepen our sense of where we are called and sent.

Vocation and Prayer

Lent is a time of focused prayer. Christians often take on a particular spiritual discipline as a Lenten practice, but prayer is always the heart of this season of preparation. Whatever people identify as their vocation—relationships, work, family, service, or other commitments—any true calling is sustained by prayer. The way of vocation is long and winding, not unlike the forty days of Lent. So spending more time in prayer during this season can deepen our sense of vocation and our clarity about what we are—and are not—called to be or do as followers of Christ.

EASTER

Resurrection Changes Everything

Christian callings are shaped by the paschal mystery: we die to self and rise to new life. Jesus's passion and resurrection created the model for our own daily living. When we respond to any call to serve others, we eventually have to let go of our desire for control in order for the calling to flourish. So every vocation not only involves sacrifice but also powerful transformation for good. Exploring the role of suffering in vocation, the reality of unexpected (or unwanted) callings, and the evolution of a calling over time can be life changing for people in your congregation who are struggling with what God seems to be asking from their lives right now.

I Tell You the Truth

Witness is at the heart of Easter. From the Gospel stories of the women who discovered the empty tomb to the new calling given to the disciples who were charged to spread the good news of Christ's death and resurrection, Easter is a season to remember how the call to witness is given to every follower of Christ. Inviting people to give a testimony to what God has done in their lives can be a powerful preaching moment in the Easter season—connecting faith and daily life, worship and work. Whether this witness is given within worship, referenced in the sermon, or offered during a panel discussion outside worship, Easter can provide a reminder to listen to each other share good news of what we have learned about God at work in our lives and world.

Christ and Our Callings

"Who do you say that I am?" Jesus asks his followers. What do our beliefs about Christ mean for our vocations? The person of Jesus matters for all who call themselves Christian—and by extension, for their callings as well. Both the humanity and the divinity of

Jesus are at the heart of the Gospel narratives surrounding the Easter events, and so this season offers a moment to examine what we believe about Jesus Christ and the impact of his life, message, and mission on our own. The heart of the Easter story involves challenging questions of suffering, sacrifice, and salvation. We wrestle with the truth and meaning of these theological conundrums today as much as the early Christians did, but wrestling is part of any faithful calling. Studying the portrayal of Jesus by each Gospel writer offers a wide array of perspectives on the person of Jesus—multiple lenses through which to consider our callings from God.

SEASON AFTER PENTECOST

Vocation and the Spirit

What role does the Holy Spirit play in our callings? Throughout Scripture, the Spirit of God is closely tied to God's work as creator, caller, and comforter. Other scriptural images evoked during Pentecost—burning fire, breath of life, and speaking in new languages—can connect to the passion and reawakening of discovering a new vocation. Pentecost can be an invigorating season to see our callings with fresh eyes: What restlessness might be leading us somewhere new? How can vocation's demands be a refining fire? Where are we hearing God speak in new ways today?

Vocation and the Church

Who are we as church? How is vocation a communal reality? We share a common calling as Christians to follow Christ with our whole lives—our primary vocation. We also believe that we live out our particular callings with others and for others. Vocations arise out of community and call forth people's service back to the community. The season following Easter may be a ripe time for rediscovery or recommitment to your congregation's sense of calling as a community and its commitment to support the vocations of each member.

Vocation and God's Mission

What does it mean to be sent forth today? To share in the mission of the church? To participate in the purposes of God for the world? What is our relationship to the culture around us? How do we remain faithful yet open to the movement of the Spirit? What happens when we encounter conflict, division, corruption, or evil as a church? Vocation is a part of these important conversations. Callings are the great commissions in our lives: the places and people to whom we are sent.

Appendix

Resources from the Collegeville Institute Seminars

To Bless Our Callings draws from the work of the Collegeville Institute Seminars, an ecumenical research project in practical theology that brings together theologians, ministers, and social scientists to explore important issues facing today's Christian communities (http://collegevilleinstitute.org/the-seminars/). Generously funded by a grant from the Lilly Endowment, Inc., the Seminars are a project of the Collegeville Institute located at Saint John's University in Collegeville, Minnesota. Since 2009 three Seminars have explored the concept of calling in order to develop a more robust theology of vocation and create resources for congregations, seminaries, universities, and other places of ministry: the Seminar on Vocation and Faith in the Professions, the Seminar on Vocation across the Lifespan, and the Seminar on Interfaith Perspectives on Vocation. The Seminars have produced a number of books and resources on vocation, including the following.

ACADEMIC BOOKS

Cahalan, Kathleen A., and Bonnie Miller-McLemore, eds. *Calling All Years Good: Christian Vocation throughout Life's Seasons*. Grand Rapids: Eerdmans, 2017.

Cahalan, Kathleen A., and Douglas J. Schuurman, eds. *Calling in Today's World: Voices from Eight Faith Traditions*. Grand Rapids: Eerdmans, 2016.

BOOKS FOR A GENERAL AUDIENCE

Cahalan, Kathleen A. *The Stories We Live: Finding God's Calling All Around Us.* Grand Rapids: Eerdmans, 2017.

Cahalan, Kathleen A., and Laura Kelly Fanucci. *Living Your Discipleship: 7 Ways to Express Your Deepest Calling*. New London, CT: Twenty-Third Publications, 2015.

RESOURCES FOR A GENERAL AUDIENCE

Called to Life (www.called-to-life.com) and *Called to Work* (www.called-to-work.com) are six-week programs for small groups to explore God's call in their lives and professional work. Free guides for participants and facilitators are available online.

Lives Explored (www.lives-explored.com) is a video storytelling project on how people experience God's call in their life, work, and relationships. Videos from different lifespan stages, professional backgrounds, and faith perspectives can be used as conversation starters for small groups or for personal reflection.

Permissions

Scripture quotations are from New Revised Standard Version Bible, copyright © 1989 by the National Council of the Churches of Christ in the United States of America. Used by permission. All rights reserved worldwide. http://nrsvbibles.org/.

"Three Choices" copyright © 2011 by Amy Ludwig VanDerwater. Originally published on poemfarm.com. Reprinted by permission of Curtis Brown, Ltd.

"Changing" copyright © 2012 by Amy Ludwig VanDerwater. Originally published on poemfarm.com. Reprinted by permission of Curtis Brown, Ltd.

"Christ, Protector of the Children," "God of Ages," "God Of Work," "Worship then Service," and "The Way, The Truth, The Life" from *Hymns for All Seasons* by Jocelyn Marshall. Copyright © 2007 by Jocelyn Marshall. http://jocelynmarshall.org/hymns.html. Used with permission.

"God of Generations" by Carolyn Winfrey Gillette. Copyright © 1998 by Carolyn Winfrey Gillette. All rights reserved. Used with permission. bcgillette@comcast.net. www.carolynshymns.com.

"For Young People," "For the Middle-Aged," "For those giving care to a patient with Alzheimer's disease," "A Litany of Thanksgiving," "Morning Prayer 1," "For those in medical services," and "For Those in Business" from *Book of Common Worship* by the Presbyterian Church (U.S.A.). Copyright © 1993 by Westminster/John Knox Press. Used with permission.

"A Contemporary Prayer for Admission to the Community of Drivers" by Rev. Daniel Benedict. Copyright © Discipleship Ministries. http://UMCdiscipleship.org. Used by permission.

"Graduating from High School," "Going to College," "Joining the Workforce," "Going on a Pilgrimage," "Beginning a New Job," "Moving from the Family Home," "Taking on the Care of Elder Parents," "Ending a Job," "Retiring," "Becoming a Grandparent or Great-Grandparent," excerpt from "Farewell to a Home," and "Celebrating a Wedding Anniversary" from *Changes: Prayers and Services Honoring Rites of Passage* by the Episcopal Church. Copyright © 2007 by the Church Pension Fund. Used with permission.

"Camp Blessing" from http://www.losd.org/resources.html by Lutherans Outdoors in South Dakota. Used with permission.

"Start Close In" from *River Flow: New & Selected Poems*, revised edition, by David Whyte. Copyright © 2012, Many Rivers Press, Langley, WA USA. Printed with permission from Many Rivers Press, www.davidwhyte.com.

"The Journey" from *Dream Work*, copyright © 1986 by Mary Oliver. Used by permission of Grove/Atlantic, Inc. Any third party use of this material, outside of this publication, is prohibited.

"There Are Many Ways Of Sharing" by Carolyn Winfrey Gillette. Copyright © 2004 Carolyn Winfrey Gillette. All rights reserved. Used with permission. bcgillette@comcast.net. www.carolynshymns.com.

"We Are Called" by David Haas. Copyright © 1988, GIA Publications, Inc. 7404 S. Mason Ave., Chicago, IL 60638. www.giamusic.com. 800.442.1358. All rights reserved. Used by permission.

"Anthem" (81251) by Tom Conry. Copyright © 1978 by Tom Conry and OCP, 5536 NE Hassalo, Portland, OR 97213. All rights reserved. Used with permission. "Prayer for Worship" by Katie Sexton. Copyright © 2011 by the Disciples of Christ Home Mission's Young Adult Commission. Used with permission.

"The Road Ahead" from "The Love of Solitude" from *Thoughts in Solitude* by Thomas Merton. Copyright © 1958 by the Abbey of Our Lady of Gethsemani. Copyright renewed 1986 by the Trustees of the Thomas Merton Legacy Trust. Reprinted by permission of Hill and Wang, a division of Farrar, Strauss and Giroux.

"A Travel Blessing" from *Common Prayer: A Liturgy for Common Radicals* by Shane Claiborne and Jonathan Wilson-Hartgrove. Copyright © 2012 by The Simple Way and School for Conversion. Use by permission of Zondervan. www.zondervan.com.

"Those who live alone," "Those entering retirement," "Teachers," and "Affirmation of Christian Vocation" from *Evangelical Lutheran Worship* by the Evangelical Lutheran Church in America. Copyright © 2006 by the Evangelical Lutheran Church in America. Used with permission.

"For the parents," excerpt from "A Thanksgiving for the Birth or Adoption of a Child," "24. For Vocation in Daily Work," "For the Unemployed," "22. For Social Service," "19. For Rogation Days (II. For commerce and industry)," "39. For those who Influence Public Opinion," and "23. For Education" from *The Book of Common Prayer* by the Episcopal Church. Public domain.

"You keep us waiting" from *A Wee Worship Book*. Copyright © 1999, 2015, WGRG, Iona Community, Scotland. GIA Publications, Inc., exclusive North American agent. All rights reserved. Used by permission.

"Things to Watch Out For" by Marlene Muller. Copyright © 2016 by Marlene Muller. Used with permission.

"Patient Trust" by Pierre Teilhard de Chardin, SJ from *Hearts on Fire: Praying with Jesuits* by Michael Harter, SJ, ed. Used with permission.

"In the Lord I'll Be Ever Thankful" by Taizé. Copyright © 1986, Ateliers et Presses de Taizé, Taizé Community, France. GIA Publications, Inc., exclusive North American agent. All rights reserved. Reprinted by permission.

"Here I Am, Lord" (80670) by Dan Schutte. Text and music © 1981 by OCP, 5536 NE Hassalo, Portland, OR 97213. All rights reserved. Used with permission.

"The Summons" by John L. Bell. Copyright © 1987, WGRG, Iona Community, Scotland. GIA Publications, Inc., exclusive North American agent. All rights reserved. Used by permission.

"The Pilgrimage of Life" from *The Book of a Thousand Prayers* by Angela Ashwin. Copyright © 1996, 2002 by Angela Ashwin. Use by permission of Zondervan. www.zondervan.com.

"Vocare Prayer" (traditional). In public domain.

"Archbishop Oscar Romero Prayer: A Step Along The Way" by Bishop Ken Untener. Copyright with permission of Little Books of the Diocese of Saginaw, Inc., based on the writings of Bishop Ken Untener.

"A Prayer for Family Life." Copyright © The Archbishops' Council. Used by permission. Copyright@churchofengland.org.

"God who is with us" by Ulla Monberg from *The Book of a Thousand Prayers* by Angela Ashwin. Copyright © Ulla Monberg. Used with permission of author.

"The Furnace of God's Love" and "Beyond Ourselves" from *Power Lines: Celtic Prayers about Work* by David Adam. Copyright © 1992 by David Adam. Used with permission.

"Prayer for People who are Separated," excerpt from "For Older People," and excerpt from "Our Commitments" from *Prayer Reflections for Group Meetings: A Parish and Ministry Resource* by Donal Harrington. Copyright © 2004 by Donal Harrington. Used with permission.

"Almighty God, your Holy Spirit equips the church" and "Almighty God, you have called us to labor in your vineyard" from *Lutheran Book of Worship: Occasional Services.* Copyright © 1982 by Association of Evangelical Lutheran Churches, Lutheran Church in America, The American Lutheran Church, and The Evangelical Lutheran Church in Canada. Used with permission.

Excerpt from "The Farm" from *A Timbered Choir: The Sabbath Poems 1979–1997* by Wendell Berry. Copyright © 1988 by Wendell Berry. Reprinted by permission of Counterpoint.

"Litany" from "Resources for Celebrating People Who Have Lived Long Lives" by Discipleship Ministries of the United Methodist Church. Copyright © Discipleship Ministries. http://UMCdiscipleship.org. Used by permission.

"Prayer before a Meeting" from *Prayer for Parish Groups: Preparing and Leading Prayer for Group Meetings* by Donal Harrington and Julie Kavanagh. Copyright © 1998 by Donal Harrington and Julie Kavanagh. Used by permission of the publisher.

"We Look with Uncertainty" from *The Dancing Animal Woman: A Celebration of Life* by Anne Hillman. Copyright © 1994 by Anne Hillman. www.annehillman.net. Used with permission.

"God, We Spend a Lifetime Growing" by Carolyn Winfrey Gillette. Copyright © 2001 Carolyn Winfrey Gillette. All rights reserved. Used with permission. bcgillette@comcast.net. www.carolynshymns.com.

"For Each Day of Life We Thank Thee." Words: H. Glen Lanier. © 1976 The Hymn Society (Admin. Hope Publishing Company, Carol Stream, IL 60188). All rights reserved. Used by permission.

"Invocation #1," "Call to Worship," and "Invocation" by Caring Ministries of the Church of the Brethren. Copyright © Caring Ministries of the Church of the Brethren. Reprinted with permission of Brethren Press (www.brethrenpress.com).

"A prayer of thanksgiving," "For daily life," "From the highway and from the skies," "For everyone who works," "For those who give time without financial compensation," "Lord, your love has brought us here," "For work," "For those in law enforcement and social services," and "For those in banking, business, and service industries" from *Worship & Daily Life: A Resource for Worship Planners*. Copyright © 1999 Discipleship Resources, Nashville, TN. All rights reserved. Used by permission.

"30. Clerical or Support Staff," "71. Administrator, Manager, or Coordinator," "36. Fine or Applied Artist," "27. Builder," "29. Business Owner," "23. For a Caregiver Who Has Died," "77. Cook/Meal Preparation and Service Worker," "31. Doctor," "44. Police, Fire, or Emergency Worker," "33. Farmer," "45. Police, Fire, or Emergency Worker," "37. Health or Mental Health Services Provider," "38. Homemaker," "40. Judge," "41. Lawyer," "85. Musician, Choral or Instrumental," "32. Doctor," "42. Police, Fire, or Emergency Worker," "47. Public Servant or Government Employee," "48. Salesperson," "49. Scholar or Scientist," "72. Advocate for the Oppressed," "50. Teacher or Professor," "89. Service Volunteer," and "55. Writer" from *Blessed Are Those Who Mourn: Personalized Prayers of the Faithful for the Funeral Rite* by George C. Michalek and Barbara M. Fader. Copyright © 1998 by George C. Michalek and Barbara M. Fader. Used with permission of authors.

"Call Us, One and All, Together," "Hope of Our Calling: Hope through Courage Won," and "For All with Heavy Loads to Bear" by Ally Barrett. Words © Ally Barrett. Used by permission.

"Lord of Our Growing Years." Words: David Mowbray. © 1982 The Jubilate Group (Admin. Hope Publishing Company, Carol Stream, IL 60188). All rights reserved. Used by permission.

"We Enter Your Church, Lord" by Carolyn Winfrey Gillette. Copyright © 2003 by Carolyn Winfrey Gillette. All rights reserved. Used with permission. bcgillette@comcast.net. www.carolynshymns.com.

"A Hymn of Calling" by Laura Kelly Fanucci. Copyright © 2013 by Laura Kelly Fanucci. Used with permission.

"100. For Those Who Work" from *The Wideness of God's Mercy: Litanies to Enlarge Our Prayer* by Jeffery W. Rowthorn. Copyright © 1985, 1995, 2007 by Jeffery W. Rowthorn. Used with permission of publisher.

"Difficulty in vocational life, unemployment" from *Evangelical Lutheran Worship Pastoral Care* by Evangelical Lutheran Church in America. Copyright © 2008 by the Evangelical Lutheran Church in America. Used with permission.

"Morning Prayers" from *The Worshipbook* by Joint Committee on Worship, Cumberland Presbyterian Church, United Presbyterian Church in the U.S.A, and Presbyterian Church in the U.S. Copyright © 1970, 1972 by the Westminster Press. Used with permission.

"O God, our Creator, You Work Every Day" by Carolyn Winfrey Gillette. Copyright © 2000 by Carolyn Winfrey Gillette. All rights reserved. Used with permission. bcgillette@comcast.net. www.carolynshymns.com.

"The Son of God, Our Christ." Words: Edward M. Blumenfeld. © 1957, Ren. 1985 The Hymn Society (Admin. Hope Publishing Company, Carol Stream, IL 60188). All rights reserved. Used by permission.

"O Grant Us, God, a Little Space" (1870, alt.) by John Ellerton, public domain.

"Blessing of Healing Hands" by The Catholic Health Association of the United States. Copyright © 2016 by The Catholic Health Association of the United States. Used with permission.

"Thanksgiving for All Who Work in Science and Technology" by Olivia Masih White. Copyright © 2017 Local Church Ministries, Faith Formation Ministry Team, United Church of Christ, 700 Prospect Avenue, Cleveland, OH 44115–1100. Permission granted to reproduce or adapt this material for use in services of worship or church education. All publishing rights reserved. Used with permission.

"For Caregivers and Others in Support of the Sick" from *Enriching Our Worship 2: Ministry with the Sick or Dying; Burial of a Child* by Episcopal Church. Copyright © 2000 by The Church Pension Fund. Used with permission.

Bibliography of Cited Sources

Adam, David. *Power Lines: Celtic Prayers about Work*. Harrisburg, PA: Morehouse, 2000.

Anderson, Vienna Cobb. *Prayers of Our Hearts in Word and Action*. New York: Crossroad, 1991.

The Anglican Church in Aotearoa, New Zealand and Polynesia. *A New Zealand Prayer Book / He Karakia Mihinare o Aotearoa*. San Francisco: HarperCollins, 1997.

Archbishops' Council, Church of England. "A Prayer for Family Life." https://www.churchofengland.org/prayer-worship/topical-prayers/prayers-for-children-and-families.aspx.

Ashwin, Angela, ed. *The Book of a Thousand Prayers*. Grand Rapids: Zondervan, 2002.

Barrett, Ally. "Hymns." May 2017. https://reverendally.org/reverendallys-hymns/.

Batastini, Robert J., and Michael A. Cymbala, eds. *Gather*. 2nd ed. Chicago: GIA, 1994.

Batastini, Robert J., et al. *Worship: A Hymnal and Service Book for Roman Catholics*. 3rd ed. Chicago: GIA, 1986.

Bell, John L. "The Summons." In *Gather*, edited by Robert J. Batastini and Michael A. Cymbala, hymn 510. Chicago: GIA, 1994.

Benedict, Daniel. "Rite of Passage for Teens Receiving Their Drivers' Licenses." Discipleship Ministries. https://www.umcdiscipleship.org/resources/rite-of-passage-prayers-for-teens-receiving-their-drivers-licenses.

Berry, Wendell. "The Farm." In *A Timbered Choir: The Sabbath Poems 1979–1997*, 141. Washington, DC: Counterpoint, 1998.

Blumenfeld, Edward M. "The Son of God, Our Christ." In *Evangelical Lutheran Worship*, Evangelical Lutheran Church in America, hymn 584. Minneapolis: Augsburg Fortress, 2006.

Calvert, Mary. *God to Enfold Me: A Retreat in the Celtic Tradition*. Pinner, UK: Grail, 1993.

Caring Ministries of the Church of the Brethren. "Calls to Worship, Invocations, Litany," 2009. http://www.brethren.org/family/documents/calls-to-worship.pdf.

———. "The Journey," 2003. http://www.brethren.org/family/documents/journey.pdf.

Catholic Health Association of the United States. "Blessing of Healing Hands." https://www.chausa.org/docs/default-source/prayers/blessing-of-healing-hands.pdf.

———. "A Blessing for Health Care Leaders." https://www.chausa.org/docs/default-source/prayers/a-blessing-for-health-care-leaders.pdf.

Claiborne, Shane, and Jonathan Wilson-Hartgrove. *Common Prayer: A Liturgy for Ordinary Radicals.* Grand Rapids: Zondervan, 2012.

Conry, Tom. "Anthem." In *Gather*, edited by Robert J. Batastini and Michael A. Cymbala, hymn 494. Chicago: GIA, 1994.

Discipleship Ministries of the United Methodist Church. "Resources for Celebrating People Who Have Lived Long Lives." https://www.umcdiscipleship.org/resources/resources-for-celebrating-people-who-have-lived-long-lives.

Ellerton, John. "O Grant Us, God, a Little Space." In *The New Century Hymnal*, edited by James W. Crawford, Arthur G. Clyde, and United Church of Christ, hymn 516. Cleveland: Pilgrim, 1995.

Episcopal Church. *The Book of Common Prayer.* New York: Church Publishing, 1979.

———. *Changes: Prayers and Service Honoring Rites of Passage.* New York: Church Publishing, 2007.

———. *Enriching Our Worship 2: Ministry with the Sick or Dying; Burial of a Child.* New York: Church Publishing, 2000.

Episcopal Diocese of Alabama. "Vocare Prayer" (traditional). http://www.dioala.org/vocare/vocare.html.

Episcopal Diocese of Los Angeles. "Collect and Prayers," October 2009. http://www.episcopalchurch.org/library/document/collect-and-prayers-older-adults.

Evangelical Lutheran Church in America. *Evangelical Lutheran Worship.* Minneapolis: Augsburg Fortress, 2006.

———. *Pastoral Care.* Minneapolis: Augsburg Fortress, 2008.

Fanucci, Laura Kelly. "A Hymn of Calling," May 29, 2013. http://collegevilleinstitute.org/bearings/prayers-and-hymns-of-calling-and-vocation/.

Gillard, Richard. "The Servant Song." In *Gather*, edited by Robert J. Batastini and Michael A. Cymbala, hymn 476. Chicago: GIA, 1994.

Gillette, Carolyn Winfrey. "God of Generations." http://carolynshymns.com/god_of_generations.html.

———. "God, We Spend a Lifetime Growing." http://www.carolynshymns.com/god_we_spend_a_lifetime_growing.html.

———. "O God, Our Creator, You Work Every Day." http://www.carolynshymns.com/o_god_our_creator_you_work_every_day.html.

———. "There Are Many Ways of Sharing." http://carolynshymns.com/there_are_many_ways_of_sharing.html.

———. "We Enter Your Church, Lord." http://www.carolynshymns.com/we_enter_your_church_lord.html.

Green, Fred Pratt. "How Clear Is Our Vocation, Lord." In *Evangelical Lutheran Worship*, Evangelical Lutheran Church in America, hymn 580. Minneapolis: Augsburg Fortress, 2006.

Haarsma, Deborah B. "The People Had a Mind to Work: A Service for the Sunday before Labor Day." *Reformed Worship* 72 (June 2004) 38.

Haas, David. "We Are Called." In *Gather*, edited by Robert J. Batastini and Michael A. Cymbala, hymn 518. Chicago: GIA, 1994.

Harrington, Donal. *Prayer Reflections for Group Meetings: A Parish and Ministry Resource*. Dublin: Columba, 2004.

Harrington, Donal, and Julie Kavanagh. *Prayer for Parish Groups: Preparing and Leading Prayer for Group Meetings*. Winona, MN: Saint Mary's, 1998.

Hillman, Anne. "We Look with Uncertainty." In *The Dancing Animal Woman: A Celebration of Life*, 215. Norfolk, CT: Bramble Books, 1994.

International Commission on English in the Liturgy. *Book of Blessings*. Collegeville, MN: Liturgical, 1992.

Joint Committee on Worship, Cumberland Presbyterian Church, United Presbyterian Church in the USA, and Presbyterian Church in the US. *The Worshipbook*. Philadelphia: Westminster, 1970.

Kerr, Hugh T. "God of Our Life." http://www.hymnary.org/text/god_of_our_life_through_all_the_circling.

Lanier, H. Glen. "For Each Day of Life We Thank Thee." http://www.hymnary.org/text/for_each_day_of_life_we_thank_thee.

Lutheran Church in America, American Lutheran Church, Evangelical Lutheran Church of Canada, and Lutheran Church—Missouri Synod. *Lutheran Book of Worship*. Minneapolis: Augsburg, 1978.

Lutherans Outdoors in South Dakota. "Camp Blessing." http://www.losd.org/resources.html.

Marshall, Jocelyn. "Christ, Protector of the Children." http://jocelynmarshall.org/texts/Protector.html.

———. "God of Ages." http://jocelynmarshall.org/texts/god_of_ages.html.

———. "God of Work." http://jocelynmarshall.org/texts/god_of_work.html.

———. "The Way, the Truth, the Life." http://jocelynmarshall.org/texts/The_Way.html.

———. "Worship Then Service." http://jocelynmarshall.org/texts/Worship.html.

Merton, Thomas. *Thoughts in Solitude*. New York: Farrar, Straus and Cudahy, 1958.

Michalek, George C., and Barbara M. Fader. *Blessed Are Those Who Mourn: Personalized Prayers of the Faithful for the Funeral Rite*. Notre Dame: Ave Maria, 1998.

Monberg, Ulla. "God Who Is With Us." In *The Book of a Thousand Prayers*, edited by Angela Ashwin, 110. Grand Rapids: Zondervan, 2002.

Mowbray, David. "Lord of Our Growing Years." In *Worship: A Hymnal and Service Book for Roman Catholics*, Robert J. Batastini et al., hymn 556. Chicago: GIA, 1986.

Muller, Marlene. "Things to Watch Out For," August 24, 2016. http://collegevilleinstitute.org/bearings/things-to-watch-out-for/.

Oliver, Mary. "The Journey." In *Dream Work*, 38–39. Boston: Atlantic Monthly, 1986.

Presbyterian Church (USA). *Book of Common Worship*. Louisville, KY: Westminster/John Knox, 1993.

Rahberg, Samuel. "Enduring Ministry: Hope." Unpublished poem.

———. "A Prayer for Christian Leaders." Unpublished prayer.

Rowthorn, Jeffery W. *The Wideness of God's Mercy*. New York: Church Publishing, 2007.

Schutte, Dan. "Here I Am, Lord." In *Gather*, edited by Robert J. Batastini and Michael A. Cymbala, hymn 492. Chicago: GIA, 1994.

Sexton, Katie. "Prayer for Worship." https://docyac.files.wordpress.com/2011/02/young-adult-week-2011-resource-packet.pdf.

Stafford, William. "The Way It Is." In *The Way It Is: New and Selected Poems*, 42. Saint Paul: Graywolf, 1998.

Struther, Jan. "Lord of All Hopefulness." In *Worship: A Hymnal and Service Book for Roman Catholics*, Robert J. Batastini et al., hymn 568. Chicago: GIA, 1986.

Taizé. "In the Lord I'll Be Ever Thankful." In *Gather*, edited by Robert J. Batastini and Michael A. Cymbala, hymn 396. Chicago: GIA, 1994.

Teilhard de Chardin, Pierre. "Patient Trust." In *Hearts on Fire: Praying with Jesuits*, edited by Michael Harter, 58. Chestnut Hill, MA: Institute of Jesuit Sources, 1993.

Thurman, Howard. "How Good to Center Down!" In *Meditations of the Heart*, 28–29. Boston: Beacon, 1999.

Topping, Frank, ed. *Daily Prayer*. Oxford: Oxford University Press, 2003.

Untener, Kenneth. "Archbishop Oscar Romero Prayer: A Step Along the Way." http://www.usccb.org/prayer-and-worship/prayers-and-devotions/prayers/archbishop_romero_prayer.cfm.

VanDerwater, Amy Ludwig. "Changing," January 18, 2012. http://www.poemfarm.amylv.com/2012/01/changing.html.

———. "Three Choices," March 30, 2011. http://www.poemfarm.amylv.com/2011/03/poem-364-offers-three-choices.html.

White, Olivia Masih. "Thanksgiving for All Who Work in Science and Technology." http://www.ucc.org/worship/worship-ways/nlb/special-occassions/special-litany-of.html.

Whyte, David. "Start Close In." In *River Flow: New and Selected Poems*, 360–61. Rev. ed. Langley, WA: Many Rivers, 2012.

Wild Goose Worship Group. *Wee Worship Book—5th Incarnation*. Chicago: GIA, 2015.

Williams, Aileen, ed. *Worship and Daily Life: A Resource for Worship Planners*. Nashville: Discipleship Resources, 1999.

Names Index

Adam, David, 60, 69
Anderson, Vienna Cobb, 69, 120, 152
Anglican Church in Aotearoa, New Zealand and Polynesia, 87
Archbishop' Council, 55
Ashwin, Angela, 52

Barrett, Ally, 106, 108, 130
Bell, John, 50
Benedict, Daniel, 21
Berry, Wendell, 63
Blumenfeld, Edward M., 128

Calvert, Mary, 85
Caring Ministries of the Church of the Brethren, 96, 97
Catholic Health Association of the United States, 135, 148
Claiborne, Shane, 37
Conry, Tom, 33

Ellerton, John, 131
Episcopal Church, 23, 24, 26, 38, 39, 41, 56, 57, 70, 72, 85, 88, 120, 121, 138, 140, 144, 145, 147
Episcopal Diocese of Alabama, 53

Episcopal Diocese of Los Angeles, 82
Evangelical Lutheran Church in America, 39, 61, 62, 84, 121, 145, 163

Fader, Barbara M., 104
Fanucci, Laura Kelly, 111

Gillard, Richard, 66
Gillette, Carolyn Winfrey, 16, 31, 93, 109, 125
Green, Fred Pratt, 80

Haarsma, Deborah B., 164
Haas, David, 32
Harrington, Donal, 61, 86, 90, 101
Hillman, Anne, 92

International Commission on English in the Liturgy, 76, 83, 123, 137, 149, 151, 162

Joint Committee on Worship, 124

Kavanagh, Julie, 90
Kerr, Hugh T., 79

Subject Index

Subject Index

calendar celebrations, 167–84
  fall, 167–69
  spring, 171–72
  summer, 172–73
  winter, 169–70
calling. *See also* vocation
  of children, 3–4
    hymns celebrating, 14–16
    petitions for, 12
    poems speaking to, 13–14
  of later adulthood, 67–68
    hymns celebrating, 78–80
    petitions for, 76–77
    poems speaking to, 77–78
  of midlife, 51–52
    hymns celebrating, 65–66
    petitions for, 62–63
    poems speaking to, 63–64
  of older adults, 81–82
    hymns celebrating, 92–94
    petitions for, 91
    poems speaking to, 92
  seasonal themes connected
    with, 167–73
  of young adults, 34–36
    hymns celebrating, 47–50
    petitions for, 44
    poems speaking to, 45–47
  of youth, 17–18
    hymns celebrating, 31–33
    petitions for, 27
    poems speaking to, 28–31
camp, church, 11, 25–26
caregivers, 55–56, 73–74
  prayer at funerals, 102
  prayers for, 121–23, 129–30,
    145–48
child care, 10, 121–23, 145–46
child in womb, blessing for, 5
childbirth, 6
  blessing for new grandparents,
    71–72
  blessing for new parents, 41
children, 3–16

hymns celebrating, 14–16
petitions for, 12
poems speaking to, 13
prayers for, 4–11
Christian vocation, affirmation,
  162–63
Christmas, 82, 178–79
chronos (chronological time), 176
church. *See also* worship
  Bible study, 76
  committees, 61–62, 75–76,
    89–90
  Communion, welcoming
    children to, 8
  leadership, 75
  mission trips, 26
  nursery, prayer for, 10
  senior groups, 89–90
  Sunday school, 10–11
  vacation Bible school, 11
  vocation and, 183
  youth retreats, 25–26
  young adult ministry, 41–44
college
  beginning, 23–24
  graduation, 36–37
comfort, in suffering, 85
commerce, workers in, 140,
  155–56
common good, 31, 119–20, 142–43
communications workers, 151–53
Communion, welcoming children
  to, 8
confirmation, prayer for
  preparation, 24–25
congregational leadership, 61–62,
  75
congregations, work, 113
connections, creating, 133
construction workers, 148–49
  prayer at funerals, 102
counselors, 138–39
  prayer at funerals, 103
crisis, 59–60

petitions for, 91
poems speaking to, 92
prayers for, 82–90
Ordinary Time, 175–76

parents, blessing for new, 41
Pentecost, 35, 82
season after, 183–84
personal prayers, 124–25
pharmacists. *See also* doctors,
nurses
police officers, 142–44
prayer at funerals, 104
preaching on vocation, 167–84
preparation, 176
Presidents' Day, 170
professions
blessing of tools, 162
prayers for specific, 132–56
vocation and profession,
113–31
providence, 179

relatives, loss of, 74–75
religious education classes, 10–11
retail workers, 155–56
prayer at funerals, 104
retirement, 70, 76–77, 83–84

sabbath, 175
sacraments. *See also* marriage
baptism, 7, 109, 125
Communion, 8
confirmation, 24–25
salespeople, 155–56
prayer at funerals, 104
school
blessing for end of year, 21–22
high school graduation, 22–23
school, blessing for new year
for elementary students, 9
for junior high and high school
students, 19–20
scientists, 136–37

prayer at funerals, 104
scripture
Psalm 71:17–18, 1
Psalm 139:13,15, 5
Ecclesiastes 3:1–4, 165
Jeremiah 1:5, 5
Luke 2:52, 18
Luke 9:48, 10
1 Corinthians 3:9, 113
1 Samuel 3, 4
seasons of church year, 174–84
senior groups, 89–90
separation or divorce, 60–61
single life, blessing for, 39
social workers, 138
prayer at funerals, 104
stewardship, 53–54
suffering, 72–73, 74–75
by adolescents, 27
by children, 12, 14–15
comfort in, 85
summer camp, 11
Sunday school, 10–11

teachers, 10, 144–45
prayer at funerals, 104
technology, 136–37
thanksgiving, 47
litany, 97–99
prayer of, 97
in workforce rite of blessing,
159–60
Thanksgiving (holiday), 168–69
therapists, 138–39
time, *kairos* or *chronos*, 176
tools of profession, blessing of, 162
transportation industry, 149–51
travelers, 150

unemployment, 57, 120–21

vacation Bible school, 11
Valentine's Day, 170
Veterans Day, 168

Made in the USA
San Bernardino, CA
30 November 2017